# Economic Philosophy

# Economic Philosophy

## Joan Robinson

**ALDINE**TRANSACTION
A Division of Transaction Publishers
New Brunswick (U.S.A.) and London (U.K.)

Second paperbaclk printing 2009

Copyright 1962 by Joan Robinson.

Library of Congress Catalog Number: 2006048146
ISBN: 978-0-202-30908-8
Printed in the United States of America

Library of Congress Cataloging-in-Publication

Robinson, Joan, 1903-1983.
    Economic philosophy / Joan Robinson.
        p. cm.
    Originally published: Chicago : Aldine Pub. Co., c1962.
    Includes bibliographical references and index.
    Contents: Metaphysics, motals and science—The classics : value—The neo-classics : unity—The Keynesian revolution—Development and under-development—What are the rulees of the game?
        ISBN 0-202-30908-8 (pbk.)
    1. Economics. I. Title.

HB71.R6    2006                                2006048146
330.0—dc22

# CONTENTS

# I

# METAPHYSICS, MORALS AND SCIENCE

ONE reason why modern life is so uncomfortable is that we have grown self-conscious about things that used to be taken for granted. Formerly people believed what they believed because they thought it was true, or because it was what all right-thinking people thought. But since Freud exposed to us our propensity to rationalization and Marx showed how our ideas spring from ideologies we have begun to ask: Why do I believe what I believe? The fact that we ask such questions implies that we think that there is an answer to be found but, even if we could answer them at one layer, another remains behind: Why do I believe what I believe about what it is that makes me believe it? So we remain in an impenetrable fog. Truth is no longer true. Evil is no longer wicked. "It all depends on what you mean." But this makes life impossible — we must find a way through.

"Backward or forward, it's just as far. Out or in, the way's as narrow." "Who are you?" "Myself. Can you say as much?" "What are you?" "The Great Boyg ... Go round about, go round about."[1]

We must go round about to find the roots of our own beliefs. In the general mass of notions and sentiments that make up an ideology those concerned with economic life play a large part, and economics itself (that is the subject as it is taught in universities and evening classes and pronounced upon in leading articles) has always been partly a vehicle for the ruling ideology of each period as well as partly a method of scientific investigation.

[1] Ibsen, *Peer Gynt*, Act II, Scene 7.

I

How can we distinguish ideology from science?

First of all we must define what we mean by definitions. It is important to avoid confusing logical definitions with natural history categories. A *point* is defined as that which has position but no magnitude. Clearly no one has ever observed a point. It is a logical abstraction. But how to define an elephant? The man had the right idea who said: I cannot define an elephant but I know one when I see it.

An ideology is much more like an elephant than like a point. It is something which exists, that we can describe and discuss and dispute about. To settle disputes it is no good appealing to a logical definition; what we need are not definitions but criteria. An elephant is a pretty clear case, but take another example — those swans which logicians are so fond of. If the word "swan" is to describe a bird that has the characteristic, amongst others, of appearing white, then those black birds in Australia must be called by another name, but if the criteria for being a swan are anatomical and do not mention colour, then the black and the white swans are in the same category. All the argument is about how to set up the categories, not about the creatures. They are what they are however we choose to label them.

What then are the criteria of an ideological proposition, as opposed to a scientific one? First, that if an ideological proposition is treated in a logical manner, it either dissolves into a completely meaningless noise or turns out to be a circular argument. Take the proposition: All men are equal. In a logical view what does it mean? The word "equal" applies to quantities. What — are all men the same weight? Or do they all get the same marks in intelligence tests? Or — to stretch the meaning of quantity a little — do I find them all equally agreeable? "Equal" without saying in what respect is just a noise. In this case, the equality is just in respect of equality. Every man is equally equal.

The hallmark of a metaphysical proposition is that it is not capable of being tested. We cannot say in what respect the world would be different if it were not true. The world would be just the same except that we would be making different noises about it. It can never be proved wrong, for it will roll out of every argument on its own circularity; it claims to be true by definition of its own terms. It purports to say something about real life, but we can learn nothing from it. Adopting Professor Popper's[1] criterion for propositions that belong to the empirical sciences, that they are capable of being falsified by evidence, it is not a scientific proposition.

Yet metaphysical statements are not without content. They express a point of view and formulate feelings which are a guide to conduct. The slogan "All men are equal" expresses a protest against privilege by birth. In an egalitarian society no one would ever have thought of saying any such thing. It expresses a moral standard for private life — that it is wrong to be snobbish about class or colour; and a programme for political life — to create a society where all have the same rights; to refuse to accept a state in which some are more equal than others.

Metaphysical propositions also provide a quarry from which hypotheses can be drawn. They do not belong to the realm of science and yet they are necessary to it. Without them we would not know what it is that we want to know. Perhaps the position is different in the respectable sciences, but, so far as the investigation of psychological and social problems is concerned, metaphysics has played an important, perhaps an indispensable, role.

Take our example — the slogan "All men are equal" provides a programme for research. Let us find out whether class or colour is correlated with the statistical distribution of innate ability. It is not an easy task, for ideology has soaked right into

[1] See *The Logic of Scientific Discovery*.

material we are to deal with. What is ability? How can we devise measurements that separate what is innate from what is due to environment? We shall have a hard struggle to eliminate ideology from the answer, but the point is that without ideology we would never have thought of the question.

2

Whether or not ideology can be eliminated from the world of thought in the social sciences, it is certainly indispensable in the world of action in social life. A society cannot exist unless its members have common feelings about what is the proper way of conducting its affairs, and these common feelings are expressed in ideology.

From the standpoint of evolution, it seems plausible to say that ideology is a substitute for instinct. The animals seem to know what to do; we have to be taught. Because the standard of proper behaviour is not passed on in the genes, it is highly malleable and comes up in all sorts of different forms in different societies, but some standard of morality is necessary for every social animal.

The biological necessity for morality arises because, for the species to survive, any animal must have, on the one hand, some egoism — a strong urge to get food for himself and to defend his means of livelihood; also — extending egoism from the individual to the family — to fight for the interests of his mate and his young. On the other hand social life is impossible unless the pursuit of self-interest is mitigated by respect and compassion for others. A society of unmitigated egoists would knock itself to pieces; a perfectly altruistic individual would soon starve. There is a conflict between contrary tendencies, each of which is necessary to existence, and there must be a set of rules to reconcile them. Moreover, there must be some mechanism to make an individual keep the rules when they conflict with his immediate advantage.

Adam Smith derives morality from feelings of sympathy —

How selfish soever man may be supposed, there are evidently some principles in his nature, which interest him in the fortune of others, and render their happiness necessary to him, though he derives nothing from it, except the pleasure of seeing it. Of this kind is pity or compassion, the emotion which we feel for the misery of others, when we either see it, or are made to conceive it in a very lively manner. That we often derive sorrow from the sorrow of others, is a matter of fact too obvious to require any instances to prove it; for this sentiment, like all the other original passions of human nature, is by no means confined to the virtuous and humane, though they perhaps may feel it with the most exquisite sensibility. The greatest ruffian, the most hardened violator of the laws of society, is not altogether without it.[1]

This is true as far as it goes but it does not cover the whole ground. When it comes to a conflict, I will save myself at your expense — sympathy will not be enough to stop me. Altruistic emotion is strong enough to evoke self-sacrifice from a mother defending her young; it is very unreliable in any other context.

Since the egoistic impulses are stronger than the altruistic, the claims of others have to be imposed upon us. The mechanism by which they are imposed is the moral sense or conscience of the individual. To take an example from the economic sphere, consider respect for the property of others. Stealing as such is not very deep in the category of wickedness. We do not feel the natural repugnance to it that we do to cruelty or meanness — except when it amounts to cruelty and meanness — the rich robbing the poor. When it is the other way round, we rather like it. When we read that a dacoit or a bandit who has been playing Robin Hood has at last been captured, our sympathy is not wholeheartedly with the police. Yet a lack of honesty is a very great nuisance in society. It is a source of expense and it is thoroughly tiresome — just as tiresome for thieves as

[1] *The Theory of Moral Sentiments*, Vol. I, pp. 1–2.

for everyone else; without honour among thieves even thieving would be impracticable.

In the absence of respect for property it would have been quite impossible to achieve a reasonable standard of life. Even the simplest investment — ploughing for next season's harvest — would not be worth while on a scale beyond what a man could guard at harvest time. To impose fear of punishment by force goes some way, but it is expensive, ineffective and vulnerable to counter-attack. Honesty is much cheaper. But observe, it is the honesty of *other people* that is necessary for *my* comfort. If all were honest except me, I should be in a very fortunate position. The necessity for each to be subject to the good of all gives rise to the need for morality. As Dr. Johnson put it —

The happiness of society depends on virtue. In Sparta theft was allowed by general consent; theft, therefore, was *there* not a crime, but then there was no security; and what a life must they have had when there was no security. Without truth there must be a dissolution of society. As it is, there is so little truth that we are almost afraid to trust our ears; but how should we be, if falsehood were multiplied ten times?[1]

Just because thieving does not arouse any strong natural repugnance, respect for the property of others has to be taught. This is a technical necessity, to make social life possible. Take an example from the rooks. They nest together sociably. Every spring the nests have to be refurbished or new built. Instinct, or whatever it is that governs behaviour, leads the rooks to go out and break twigs for building materials. They evidently have some natural propensity to work efficiently — to get the easiest and best twigs — or the job would never be done. But obviously the easiest and best twigs are those already in a nest. What prevents them from robbing each other? If each relied on the others to fetch twigs, the society would break down.

[1] Boswell, *The Life of Dr. Johnson* (Allen and Unwin's edition) Vol. II, p. 298.

It is not that they have an inborn dislike of second-hand twigs, for they freely use deserted nests for building material. Some observers maintain that thieving does occur occasionally and that when a thief is observed the other rooks mob him and drive him away.[1] It is not to the purpose to ask whether the thief feels a sense of guilt and the others a sense of righteous indignation (though it may well be so, for the emotional life of birds seems to be very like our own). The point is not concerned with the subjective feelings of the rooks. The point is that the same technical situation — social life and individual property — leads to the same result: a moral code backed up by sanctions.

Whether rooks have a conscience or not, we know that humans have. Instead of instinct that creates a set pattern men and women have a conscience that can take various imprints and so permit very varied patterns of society to flourish. A propensity to develop a conscience is in the structure of a healthy human brain. It is very similar to the propensity to learn to talk. The power to attach meanings to sounds and to utter them in appropriate contexts is latent at birth; it develops very rapidly in the first few years of life and continues, with less facility, thereafter. It varies from one individual to another and is sometimes lacking altogether. It has a peculiar location in the brain and may be lost through injury. Sometimes after an injury it is possible to re-train the brain (which contains some spare parts) and recapture a power to recognize words that had been lost. The propensity to learn a language is evidently pretty much the same in all races, but what language is learned depends upon the particular society in which a child grows up.

All this is true of the moral sense, or propensity to develop a conscience. It comes on gradually (a year or two later than

[1] Mr. G. K. Yeats doubts this, but he attributes the mobbing to a still more striking phenomenon, the neighbours turning against an adulterer. *The Life of the Rook*, pp. 31 and 38.

speech); some subnormal individuals lack it; some lose it through brain injuries, which, however, can sometimes be made good by re-training. The content of a conscience, like the particular language that is learned, depends upon the society in which the individual grows up.

Some people resent the idea that morality has a physical basis and arises out of biological necessity, as though this degraded the noblest aspect of human nature to the level of the beasts. This seems unreasonable. We all agree that mother-love is fine and admirable. (Even Freud, who was so much shocked by his discoveries about human nature, says that the love of a woman for her son is the purest of all emotions.[1]) Yet no one can deny that mother-love has a biological function or that we share it with the beasts. (Here the exception proves the rule — among the sticklebacks, it seems, the father takes charge of the young and displays the most besotted devotion, while the mother, having performed her purely physical part in procreation, dances off, like the male in other species, to enjoy a carefree life. Nature, like human societies, finds a great variety of solutions for the same technical problem.)

The biological mechanism for growing a conscience seems to operate through our emotional equipment.

Nature, when she formed man for society, endowed him with an original desire to please, and an original aversion to offend his brethren. She taught him to feel pleasure in their favourable, and pain in their unfavourable regard. She rendered their approbation most flattering and most agreeable to him for its own sake; and their disapprobation most mortifying and most offensive.[2]

Conscience is moulded in a child by his learning what is approved and disapproved by the rest of the family, but it works inwards and becomes a desire to be approved of by what

---

[1] *New Introductory Lectures*, translated by W. S. H. Sprott, pp. 171–2.
[2] Adam Smith, *Moral Sentiments*, Vol. I, p. 276.

Adam Smith calls the "man within the breast."[1] A secret shame is no doubt less painful than being found out, but it is still painful.

The sense of shame is natural and universal, but just what it is that causes shame depends upon convention. It is like the rule of the road. There has to be one, but in some countries it is "Keep to the left" and in others "Keep to the right."

In most societies, until recent times, morality has been purveyed through the medium of religion. It is by no means an easy matter to mould the individuals in a society to a harmonious pattern; religion is a useful way both of strengthening the desire of the individual to do whatever he thinks right, and of imposing a particular view of what is right. It works partly by cutting out morality and appealing to prudence or enlightened self-interest — the wicked will be punished; partly by teaching the individual to project the fear of disapproval on to an unseen being so that private shame is exposed to an ever-watchful eye; and partly by giving strength and purpose to the feeling of benevolence that "even the greatest ruffian ... is not altogether without."

Many people to whom morality was taught through the medium of religion really believe that there is no other motive for wanting to do what is right than to avoid the wrath of God: *Si dieu n'existe pas, tout est permis.* If there is no God, nothing is forbidden. This is one of the silliest things that has ever been said. If I do not believe in God it does not mean that I can safely drive on the right of the road in London or the left in Paris. It does not mean that thieves are any less nuisance to honest men or that a society infected with thieves is not involved in great expense to keep the pest under control. If a man's conscience disintegrates when he loses his faith in God, it cannot have set properly when he was young. It is still in the infantile stage of a

[1] Ibid., p. 304.

desire to be approved of by others and has not yet grown up into a sense of right and wrong.

A favourite argument nowadays, of the supporters of organized religion, is that it is necessary to good conduct and social harmony. The decay of religion is blamed for the crime waves, the broken homes, the strife and ill-will that torment the modern world. A return to the churches would bring a return to good order. Those who argue in this way are un-wittingly supporting the above argument. Morality is desired and respected for its own sake; religion is being recommended to us because it supports morality, not morality because it derives from religion.

Those who have no religious beliefs, on the other hand, are often inclined to try to derive moral feeling from reason. The commonest argument is that each individual ought to do right because, if he does not, others will not either. This is based on a confusion. It is the confusion of the war-time posters: "It all depends on you." Of course the authorities wanted us each to act as if we believed it. But it just was not true. Any one indi-vidual, as an individual, does not carry any appreciable weight. Of course, if his example is influential, he carries the weight that his influence brings, but the poster was not pointing at influential people. It was meant to apply one by one to the men in the street.

Take the example of voting. On a small committee it may often happen that one vote is decisive; then it is only reasonable for me to be sure to turn up to a meeting at which a decision will be taken that I happen to care about. But suppose that I live in a safe constituency, why should I vote at a general election? One vote more or less will not affect anything at all. "Ah, if everyone thought that, democracy would collapse." Yes, but I am not everyone — I am only me. The others will carry on without me. "What a shocking way to talk!" Yes, that is just the point. It is certainly right that everyone should feel that it is his duty to vote, but he cannot be persuaded by reason. He must think it is right because it is right.

Or take the rooks again. If one sneaked a twig from another's nest, just once, the system would not collapse. If he were seen and not attacked, standards would decline; but if he was unobserved? What harm would it do? There cannot be any reason not to do it except that it is not done.

More sophisticated systems seek to derive morality from the tendency of the direction of evolution. But this is not convincing. If I say: "Let evolution look after itself; I will do as I please," how can you answer me except by an appeal to my sense of duty? Evolution, certainly, accounts for my having one, but if evolution had endowed me, not only with a sense of duty, but with a knowledge of what my duty is, there would be no need to have a theory about it.

The upshot of the argument is that moral feelings are not derived from theology or from reason. They are a separate part of our equipment, like our ability to learn to talk.

If this is granted, it leaves open the question of what is the content of our ethical feelings. All the philosophical systems of ethics are attempts to give a rational account of ethical feeling; not of the fact that we have such feelings, but of what code of behaviour is based upon them.

Keynes took up the study of the theory of probability under the influence of Moore's ethical system, which taught "the obligation so to act as to produce by causal connexion the most probable maximum of eventual good through the whole procession of future ages."[1] It was a matter of the highest concern to be able to calculate probabilities. But even if Keynes had got the theory of probability right, it would not have provided a very handy manual for conducting daily life.

Other rational systems of ethics may be less fanciful, but they are no better. Professor Braithwaite points out the difference

[1] Keynes, *Two Memoirs*, p. 97.

between a system of scientific laws and a system of ethical
principles —

Alas, there is a logical difference between the two hierarchies: in
ascending the scientific hierarchy the propositions become stronger
and stronger so that we are saying more and more; in ascending the
hierarchy of ends the propositions become weaker and weaker so that
we are saying less and less. ... This arises from the fact that, whereas a
lower-level scientific law is a logical consequence of its higher-level
explanation, conversely pursuit of a wider end B is a logical consequence of pursuit of a narrower end A (together with the fact that A is
subsumed under B, i.e. that all pursuits of A are also pursuits of B). So
as we ascend the hierarchy the ends increase in content and lose all
definite outline. ... This accounts for the peculiar elusiveness that
many of us find in concepts which the great moral philosophers have
proposed as ultimate ends — Aristotle's *eudaimonia* or Mill's "happiness," for example. It is easy to give positive or negative instances of
these; but the concepts themselves seem inscrutable — almost as
inscrutable as the indefinable "goodness" of *Principia Ethica*. The
reason would seem to be that, in order to justify lesser goods, they
have to be so comprehensive as to lose all cognitive content.[1]

Reason will not help. The ethical system implanted in each
of us by our upbringing (even a rebel is influenced by what he
rebels against) was not derived from any reasonable principles;
those who conveyed it to us were rarely able to give any rational
account of it, or indeed to formulate it explicitly at all. They
handed on to us what society had taught to them, in the same
way as they handed on to us the language that they had
learned to speak.

The contents of ethical codes, comparing one society with
another, are not perhaps quite as various as their languages,
but they certainly vary a great deal.

The morality of *Hamlet* is usually taken to be a confusion
between Christian and pagan notions; it can also be seen as

[1] R. B. Braithwaite, "Moral Principles and Inductive Policies," *Proceedings
of the British Academy*, 1950, last page.

Shakespeare's imaginative insight grasping the point of view of a recently converted people who take all the business of Heaven and Hell quite literally, but retain their own ethics of the honourable duty of revenge. A proper revenge requires that an adversary should be slain in such a way as to ensure his going to Hell. The theology, perhaps, is rather naïve, but the ethical system is quite straightforward, as yet untainted by Christian feeling.

Or, to take an example more closely connected to economic behaviour, consider the Thugs. They were a sect, recruited both from Moslems and Hindus, whose religious devotions, dedicated to the Goddess Kali, consisted in strangling wayfarers in a particular ritual manner, and dividing their goods amongst the party according to a particular formula. Their code forbade them to murder women, and when once a party, for fear of leaving a witness, defied the rule, Kali deserted them and the British-Indian police found them out.

Any economic system requires a set of rules, an ideology to justify them, and a conscience in the individual which makes him strive to carry them out.

These examples recall what a variety of moulds the human conscience is capable of taking. They also demonstrate another point — that we make moral judgments of moral systems. *Hamlet* is perhaps an arguable case, but we agree about the Thugs. We may admire the discipline, the resolution and the piety of an individual Thug, but we do not approve of Thuggee as an economic system. Perhaps, dear reader, you will say that you do not disapprove, that your attitude to society is morally neutral and that any system of ethics is just another system of ethics. But would it really be true? Are you sure that you really approve the ethical system of the Thugs?

A simple-minded person believes that he knows the difference between right and wrong — that the particular mould his own conscience has taken is the only possible one (all the more so if

his ideology came to him in the form of religious belief).
Sophisticated people recognize the great variety of ethical
systems and take a relativistic view of moral questions. But all
the same, under the relativism we believe in certain absolutes.
There are certain basic ethical feelings that we all share. We
prefer kindness to cruelty and harmony to strife; we admire
courage and respect justice. Those born without these feelings
we treat as psychopaths; a society which trains its members to
crush them we regard as a morbid growth. It is no good trying
to pretend that we can think or speak about human questions
without ethical values coming in.

Perhaps Gunnar Myrdal is too sweeping when he says
(speaking as an economist) that "our very concepts are value-
loaded" and "cannot be defined except in terms of political
valuation."[1] It is true that economic terminology is coloured.
Bigger is close to better; equal to equitable; goods sound good;
disequilibrium sounds uncomfortable; exploitation, wicked;
and sub-normal profits, rather sad. All the same, taking a
particular economic system as given, we can describe the
technical features of its operation in an objective way. But it is
not possible to describe a *system* without moral judgments
creeping in. For to look at a system from the outside implies
that it is not the only possible system; in describing it we compare it (openly or tacitly) with other actual or imagined systems.
Differences imply choices, and choices imply judgment. We
cannot escape from making judgments and the judgments that
we make arise from the ethical preconceptions that have soaked
into our view of life and are somehow printed in our brains.
We cannot escape from our own habits of thought. The Boyg
bars the way. But we can go round about. We can see what we
value, and try to see why.

It does not seem that religion has ever had much to do with
our own economic ideology. The story of an eighteenth-

1 *An International Economy*, p. 337.

century parson reading the Gospel — "How hardly shall they that have riches enter the kingdom of God" — who was heard muttering under his breath "Of course that's all nonsense," may not be true, but it is certainly life-like.

The conflict between piety and economics was satirized in the *Fable of the Bees*, which Dr. Johnson said that every young man had on his shelves in the mistaken belief that it was a wicked book. (Adam Smith classed it with the Licentious Systems.) The bees one day were smitten with virtue, and began to lead a sober life, eschewing pomp and pride, and adopting frugal, modest ways. The result was a dreadful slump.

In their flourishing state,

> The Root of Evil, Avarice,
> That damn'd ill-natur'd baneful Vice,
> Was Slave to Prodigality,
> That noble Sin; whilst Luxury
> Employ'd a Million of the Poor,
> And odious Pride a Million more:
> Envy itself, and Vanity,
> Were Ministers of Industry;
> Their darling Folly, Fickleness,
> In Diet, Furniture, and Dress,
> That strange ridic'lous Vice, was made
> The very Wheel that turned the Trade.[1]

After they turn'd virtuous,

> As Pride and Luxury decrease,
> So by degrees they leave the Seas.
> Not Merchants now, but Companies
> Remove whole Manufactories.
> All Arts and Crafts neglected lie;
> Content, the Bane of Industry,
> Makes 'em admire their homely Store,
> And neither seek nor covet more.[2]

[1] Mandeville, *The Fable of the Bees* (Kaye's edition), Vol. I, p. 25.
[2] Ibid., p. 34.

Keynes' interpretation of Mandeville in terms of the theory of effective demand was somewhat forced.[1] That the luxury of the rich gives employment to the poor was something pretty obvious. In an underdeveloped country, as Mandeville's England was, there is a plentiful reserve of labour in agriculture to supply lackeys and handicraftsmen who can draw sustenance from luxury expenditure. It was a favourite theme of Dr. Johnson (who entirely agreed with Mandeville's economics though he did not accept his "monastick morality").

You cannot spend money in luxury without doing good to the poor. Nay, you do more good to them by spending it in luxury than by giving it; for by spending it in luxury you make them exert industry, whereas by giving it you keep them idle. I own, indeed, there may be more virtue in giving it immediately in charity than in spending it in luxury; though there may be pride in that too.[2]

and

Many things which are false are transmitted from book to book, and gain credit in the world. One of these is the cry against the evil of luxury. Now the truth is, that luxury produces much good. Take the luxury of building in London. Does it not produce real advantage in the conveniency and elegance of accommodation, and this all from the exertion of industry? People will tell you, with a melancholy face, how many builders are in gaol. It is plain they are in gaol, not for building; for rents are not fallen. A man gives half a guinea for a dish of green peas. How much gardening does this occasion? How many labourers must the competition to have such things early in the market, keep in employment? You will hear it said, very gravely "Why was not the half-guinea, thus spent in luxury, given to the poor? To how many might it have afforded a good meal?" Alas! has it not gone to the *industrious* poor, whom it is better to support than the *idle* poor? You are much surer that you are doing good when you *pay* money to those who work, as the recompence of their labour, than when you *give* money merely in charity. Suppose the ancient luxury

[1] *General Theory*, Chap. 23, VII.
[2] Boswell, *The Life of Dr. Johnson* (Allen & Unwin edition), Vol. II, p. 298.

of a dish of peacock's brains were to be revived; how many carcases would be left to the poor at a cheap rate? And as to the rout that is made about people who are ruined by extravagance, it is no matter to the nation that some individuals suffer. When so much general productive exertion is the consequence of luxury, the nation does not care though there are debtors in gaol; nay, they would not care though their creditors were there too.[1]

Mandeville's point was not to establish this view of economics but rather, taking it for granted, to use it to show up the double standard of a people, purporting to be Christian, who value wealth and national glory above all.

In the prose composition that he appended to the *Fable* he explains —

When I say that societies cannot be raised to wealth and power, and the top of earthly glory without vices, I do not think that by so saying, I bid men be vicious, any more than I bid them be quarrelsome or covetous, when I affirm that the profession of the law could not be maintained in such numbers and splendour, if there was not abundance of too selfish and litigious people.[2]

And he sets up an Epicure to raise objections.

He will quote my Lord Shaftesbury against me, and tell me that people may be virtuous and sociable without self-denial; that it is an affront to virtue to make it inaccessible, that I make a bugbear of it to frighten men from it as a thing impracticable; but that for his part he can praise God, and at the same time enjoy his creatures with a good conscience.

He will ask me at last, whether the legislature, the wisdom of the nation itself, while they endeavour as much as possible to discourage profaneness and immorality, and promote the glory of God, do not openly profess, at the same time, to have nothing more at heart, than the ease and welfare of the subject, the wealth, strength, honour, and what else is called the true interest of the country; and, moreover,

---

[1] Ibid., pp. 133-4.
[2] Op. cit., p. 231 (spelling modernized).

whether the most devout and most learned of our prelates in their greatest concern for our conversion, when they beseech the Deity to turn their own as well as our hearts, from the world and all carnal desires, do not in the same prayer as loudly solicit him to pour all earthly blessings and temporal felicity, on the kingdom they belong to ...

As to the two last questions, I own they are very puzzling: To what the Epicure asks, I am obliged to answer in the affirmative; and unless I would (which God forbid!) arraign the sincerity of kings, bishops, and the whole legislative power, the objection stands good against me: all I can say for myself is, that in the connexion of the facts, there is a mystery past human understanding.[1]

Adam Smith did not like it. His reply is rather flat and feeble after Mandeville's sharp satire.[2]

It is the great fallacy of Dr. Mandeville's book to represent every passion as wholly vicious, which is so in any degree and in any direction. It is thus that he treats every thing as vanity which has any reference, either to what are, or to what ought to be, the sentiments of others; and it is by means of this sophistry, that he establishes his favourite conclusion, that private vices are public benefits. If the love of magnificence, a taste for the elegant arts and improvements of human life, for whatever is agreeable in dress, furniture, or equipage, for architecture, statuary, painting and music, is to be regarded as luxury, sensuality, and ostentation, even in those whose situation allows, without any inconveniency, the indulgence of those passions, it is certain that luxury, sensuality, and ostentation are public benefits: since without the qualities upon which he thinks proper to bestow such opprobrious names, the arts of refinement could never find encouragement, and must languish for want of employment. Some popular ascetic doctrines, which had been current before his time, and which placed virtue in the entire extirpation and annihilation of all our passions, were the real foundation of this licentious system. It was easy for Dr. Mandeville to prove, first, that this entire conquest never actually took place among men; and secondly, that, if it was to take

[1] Ibid., pp. 234–5.
[2] *Moral Sentiments*, Vol. II, pp. 302–3.

place universally, it would be pernicious to society, by putting an end to all industry and commerce, and in a manner to the whole business of human life. By the first of these propositions he seemed to prove that there was no real virtue and that what pretended to be such, was a mere cheat and imposition upon mankind; and by the second, that private vices were public benefits, since without them no society could prosper or flourish.

He admits all the same that there is something in it —

But how destructive soever this system may appear, it could never have imposed upon so great a number of persons, nor have occasioned so general an alarm among those who are the friends of better principles, had it not in some respects bordered upon the truth.[1]

Indeed Mandeville has never been answered. After more than two hundred years, Keynes is brooding over our squinting morality —

In Europe, or at least in some parts of Europe—but not, I think, in the United States of America—there is a latent reaction, somewhat widespread, against basing society to the extent that we do upon fostering, encouraging, and protecting the money-motives of individuals. A preference for arranging our affairs in such a way as to appeal to the money-motive as little as possible, rather than as much as possible, need not be entirely *a priori,* but may be based on the comparison of experiences. Different persons, according to their choice of profession, find the money-motive playing a large or a small part in their daily lives, and historians can tell us about other phases of social organization in which this motive has played a much smaller part than it does now. Most religions and most philosophies deprecate, to say the least of it, a way of life mainly influenced by considerations of personal money profit. On the other hand, most men today reject ascetic notions and do not doubt the real advantages of wealth. Moreover it seems obvious to them that one cannot do without the money-motive, and that, apart from certain admitted abuses, it does its job

[1] Loc. cit.

well. In the result the average man averts his attention from the problem, and has no clear idea what he really thinks and feels about the whole confounded matter.[1]

Schumpeter makes somewhat the same point in a different context when he argues that business men cannot command the loyalty of a people,—

With the utmost ease and grace the lords and knights metamorphosed themselves into courtiers, administrators, diplomats, politicians and into military officers of a type that had nothing whatever to do with that of the medieval knight. And—most astonishing phenomenon when we come to think of it—a remnant of that old prestige survives even to this day, and not only with our ladies.

Of the industrialist and merchant the opposite is true. There is surely no trace of any mystic glamour about him which is what counts in the ruling of men. The stock exchange is a poor substitute for the Holy Grail. We have seen that the industrialist and merchant, as far as they are entrepreneurs, also fill a function of leadership. But economic leadership of this type does not readily expand, like the medieval lord's military leadership, into the leadership of nations. On the contrary, the ledger and the cost calculation absorb and confine.

I have called the bourgeois rationalist and unheroic. He can only use rationalist and unheroic means to defend his position or to bend a nation to his will. He can impress by what people may expect from his economic performance, he can argue his case, he can promise to pay out money or threaten to withhold it, he can hire the treacherous services of a condottiere or politician or journalist. But that is all and all of it is greatly overrated as to its political value. Nor are his experiences and habits of life of the kind that develop personal fascination. A genius in the business office may be, and often is, utterly unable outside of it to say boo to a goose—both in the drawing-room and on the platform.[2]

It is precisely the pursuit of profit which destroys the prestige

---

[1] *Capitalism, Socialism and Democracy*, pp. 137–8.
[2] *Essays in Persuasion*, p. 320.

of the business man. While wealth can buy all forms of respect, it never finds them freely given.

It was the task of the economist to overcome these sentiments and justify the ways of Mammon to man. No one likes to have a bad conscience. Pure cynicism is rather rare. Even the Thugs robbed and murdered for the honour of their goddess. It is the business of the economists, not to tell us what to do, but show why what we are doing anyway is in accord with proper principles.

In what follows this theme is illustrated by reference to one or two of the leading ideas of the economists from Adam Smith onwards, not in a learned manner, tracing the development of thought, nor historically, to show how ideas arose out of the problems of each age, but rather in an attempt to puzzle out the mysterious way that metaphysical propositions, without any logical content, can yet be a powerful influence on thought and action.

3

Economics is not only a branch of theology. All along it has been striving to escape from sentiment and to win for itself the status of a science. We saw above how metaphysical propositions not only express moral feelings, but also provide hypotheses. Before going on with the argument we must pause to consider how this comes about.

Scientific method is another kind of elephant — something which exists and can be described, not defined. A common view about the origin of scientific generalizations is that they are based on induction from observed instances. We used to be told that people in the Northern hemisphere arrive at the generalization: All swans are white, by a process of induction — all the swans ever seen were white, until Australia was discovered and black swans upset the generalization. This does not seem to accord with experience. The first time you see a swan, in

England, you observe that it is white, has a long neck and so forth, and you learn that it is called a swan. There is no induction about it. You generalize that swans are like that from the very first instance. Now it happens that we classify species by anatomy, not colour. To say that all swans have long necks is a circular statement, for if this creature did not have a long neck it would not be classified as a swan. If they happened to have been named Whitebirds it would have sounded silly to say black Whitebirds and those in Australia would have been called by a different name.

Another favourite conundrum that is supposed to illustrate induction, is: Why do you believe that the sun will rise tomorrow? For purposes of daily life we take it for granted; we do not believe anything about it, one way or the other. When we seriously ask: Do we believe it? and if so, why? the answer is certainly not because of induction from its past behaviour. We have a theory of the motion of the planets, which causes the apparent movement of the sun, and there is no reason to expect the process to be interrupted before tomorrow (though of course it might be — you never know). Before that there was a theory that God had created the sun to light the world and instructed it to move round, so that we could get some sleep at night. And before that there was a theory that Apollo drove his chariot daily over the sky. Before science began, there were already plenty of theories. The process of science, as Professor Popper maintains, consists in trying to *disprove* theories. The corpus of science at any moment consists of the theories that have not been disproved.

The great difficulty in the social sciences (if we may presume to call them so) of applying scientific method, is that we have not yet established an agreed standard for the disproof of an hypothesis. Without the possibility of controlled experiment, we have to rely on interpretation of evidence, and interpretation involves judgment; we can never get a knock-down answer.

But because the subject is necessarily soaked in moral feelings, judgment is coloured by prejudice.

> He who's convinced against his will
> Is of the same opinion still.

The way out of this impasse is not to shed prejudice and approach the problem to be discussed with a purely objective mind. Anyone who says to you: "Believe me, I have no prejudices," is either succeeding in deceiving himself or trying to deceive you. Professor Popper criticizes the method of argument which pretends to be based upon the impartiality of the social scientists. The objectivity of science arises, not because the individual is impartial, but because many individuals are continually testing each other's theories. "In order to avoid speaking at cross-purposes, scientists try to express their theories in such a form that they can be tested, i.e. refuted (or otherwise confirmed) by experience."[1]

I think Professor Popper is wrong in saying that the natural sciences are no better than the social sciences. They have in common the human weakness to develop patriotism for one's own work: "My theory, right or wrong!" But on top of that, in the social sciences, first, the subject-matter has much greater political and ideological content, so that other loyalties are also involved; and secondly, because the appeal to "public experience" can never be decisive, as it is for the laboratory scientists who can repeat each other's experiments under controlled conditions; the social scientists are always left with a loophole to escape through — "the consequences that have followed from the causes that I analysed are, I agree, the opposite of what I predicted, but they would have been still greater if those causes had not operated."

This need to rely on judgment has another consequence. It has sometimes been remarked that economists are more queazy

---

[1] *The Open Society and its Enemies*, Vol. II, p. 205.

and ill-natured than other scientists. The reason is that, when a writer's personal judgment is involved in an argument, disagreement is insulting.

Adam Smith remarks upon the different temperaments of poets and mathematicians —

> The beauty of poetry is a matter of such nicety, that a young beginner can scarce ever be certain that he has attained it. Nothing delights him so much, therefore, as the favourable judgments of his friends and of the public; and nothing mortifies him so severely as the contrary. The one establishes, the other shakes, the good opinion which he is anxious to entertain concerning his own performances.
>
> Mathematicians, on the contrary, who may have the most perfect assurance, both of the truth and of the importance of their discoveries, are frequently very indifferent about the reception which they may meet with from the public.
>
> ... [They] from their independency upon the public opinion, have little temptation to form themselves into factions and cabals, either for the support of their own reputation, or for the depression of that of their rivals. They are almost always men of the most amiable simplicity of manners, who live in good harmony with one another, are the friends of one another's reputation, enter into no intrigue in order to secure the public applause, but are pleased when their works are approved of, without being either much vexed or very angry when they are neglected.
>
> It is not always the same case with poets, or with those who value themselves upon what is called fine writing. They are very apt to divide themselves into a sort of literary factions; each cabal being often avowedly and almost always secretly, the mortal enemy of the reputation of every other, and employing all the mean arts of intrigue and solicitation to preoccupy the public opinion in favour of the works of its own members, and against those of its enemies and rivals.[1]

Perhaps Adam Smith had rather too exalted a view of mathematicians, and perhaps economists are not quite as bad as poets; but his main point applies. The lack of an agreed and accepted

[1] *Moral Sentiments*, Vol. I, pp. 293–7.

method for eliminating errors introduces a personal element into economic controversies which is another hazard on top of all the rest. There is a notable exception to prove the rule. Keynes was singularly free and generous because he valued no one's opinion above his own. If someone disagreed with him, it was they who were being silly; he had no cause to get peevish about it.

The personal problem is a by-product of the main difficulty, that, lacking the experimental method, economists are not strictly enough compelled to reduce metaphysical concepts to falsifiable terms and cannot compel each other to agree as to what has been falsified. So economics limps along with one foot in untested hypotheses and the other in untestable slogans. Here our task is to sort out as best we may this mixture of ideology and science. We shall find no neat answers to the questions that it raises. The leading characteristic of the ideology that dominates our society today is its extreme confusion. To understand it means only to reveal its contradictions.

# II

## THE CLASSICS: VALUE

ONE of the great metaphysical ideas in economics is expressed by the word "value." What is value and where does it come from? It does not mean usefulness — the good that goods do us.

The word VALUE, it is to be observed, has two different meanings, and sometimes expresses the utility of some particular object, and sometimes the power of purchasing other goods which the possession of that object conveys. The one may be called "value in use"; the other "value in exchange." The things which have the greatest value in use have frequently little or no value in exchange; and, on the contrary, those which have the greatest value in exchange have frequently little or no value in use. Nothing is more useful than water; but it will purchase scarce anything; scarce anything can be had in exchange for it. A diamond, on the contrary, has scarce any value in use; but a very great quantity of other goods may frequently be had in exchange for it.[1]

It does not mean market prices, which vary from time to time under the influence of casual accidents; nor is it just an historical average of actual prices. Indeed, it is not simply a price; it is something which will explain how prices come to be what they are. What is it? where shall we find it? Like all metaphysical concepts, when you try to pin it down it turns out to be just a word.

All the same, problems that have been turned up in pursuit of the causes of value are by no means empty of meaning.

[1] Adam Smith, *Wealth of Nations* (Everyman edition), Vol. I, pp. 24-5.

I

Let us recall how Adam Smith began the search —

In that early and rude state of society which precedes both the accumulation of stock and the appropriation of land, the proportion between the quantities of labour necessary for acquiring different objects, seems to be the only circumstance which can afford any rule for exchanging them for one another. If, among a nation of hunters, for example, it usually costs twice the labour to kill a beaver which it does to kill a deer, one beaver should naturally exchange for or be worth two deer. It is natural that what is usually the produce of two days' or two hours' labour, should be worth double of what is usually the produce of one day's or one hour's labour. ...

In this state of things, the whole produce of labour belongs to the labourer; and the quantity of labour commonly employed in acquiring or producing any commodity, is the only circumstance which can regulate the quantity of labour which it ought commonly to purchase, command, or exchange for.[1]

What status should be given to this proposition? It is not metaphysical — it tells a quite definite story with a perfectly factual content. It could serve as a hypothesis to be tested. But it is a hypothesis derived neither from observation nor analysis. It belongs rather to the realm of myth — a hypothesis of the same kind as that God ordered the sun to go round the earth so as to divide day from night.

Let us consider Adam Smith's theory analytically. How did it come about that the hunters wanted to trade? Exchange arises from specialization, but Adam Smith clearly intends that the forest was free for all. There was no property in special beats and he expressly excludes differences in the arduousness of work or the skill required. Why then should there be any trade? As he himself points out in a later chapter —

In that rude state of society, in which there is no division of labour, in which exchanges are seldom made, and in which every man

[1] Ibid., pp. 41-2.

provides everything for himself, it is not necessary that any stock be accumulated, or stored up before-hand, in order to carry on the business of the society. Every man endeavours to supply, by his own industry his own occasional wants, as they occur. When he is hungry, he goes to the forest to hunt; when his coat is worn out, he clothes himself with the skin of the first large animal he kills: and when his hut begins to go to ruin, he repairs it, as well as he can, with the trees, and the turf that are nearest it.[1]

How then can there be a normal price-ratio? There might be casual swaps, but why should there be regular trade at a normal price? Evidently we are to understand that, in particular transactions, the two parties agree to trade at the normal price. It is not the time that each has actually taken but the time that it "usually costs" that governs the exchange. Value rules because it is fair and right. It is after all not very far from the medieval schoolman's Just Price.

In the version of this theory that has survived to modern times, specialization is allowed; it is applied to artisans each with his special skill, owning his own means of production. This indeed accounts for exchanges, but it destroys the theory; now mere time will not serve as a measure of labours of different kinds.

The *concrete labour*, we are told, of a blacksmith produces horseshoes and of a weaver produces cloth, while *abstract labour* accounts for their value. We can find out how much abstract labour there is in each by observing their prices.

When a commodity producer brings an axe to market in order to exchange it, he finds that for his axe he can get 20 kilogrammes of grain. This means that the axe is *worth* the same amount of social labour as 20 kilogrammes of grain are worth.[2]

Even if we could make any analytical sense of this concept, it would be irrelevant from a historical point of view. For the

[1] Ibid., p. 241.

[2] *Political Economy*, a Textbook issued by the Economics Institute of the Academy of Sciences of the U.S.S.R. Laurence & Wishart, London, 1957, p. 71.

peasant economy to be viable it is necessary that each local community should support the tradesmen it requires — one blacksmith, two barbers, five priests, or whatever it may be, and they must receive a living wage per man year. Labour-time per unit of output has nothing to do with it. The simplest plan is that which still persists in an unmodernized Indian village: the village specialists have a right to a certain percentage share in the harvest and must do as much or as little work as happens to be required.

Trade and prices there have certainly been, at least since neolithic times. There is reason to believe there were travelling merchants who dealt in flint and amber and it seems fairly safe to guess that, since at each end of the journey they were selling exotic goods, outside the scheme, whatever it may have been, that ruled in the domestic market, they sold their merchandise for what it would fetch.[1] Certainly labour-time cannot have had anything to do with it.

Adam Smith's story of the beavers and deer has no warrant either analytical or historical. He derived it from moral preconceptions. That is how it ought to have been. The hunters were living in an idyllic past when the economic system was morally satisfactory.

As soon as the land of any country has all become private property the landlords, like all other men, love to reap where they never sowed, and demand a rent even for its natural produce. ...

As soon as stock has accumulated in the hands of particular persons, some of them will naturally employ it in setting to work industrious people, whom they will supply with materials and subsistence, in order to make a profit by the sale of their work, or by what their labour adds to the value of the materials.[2]

There is in every society or neighbourhood an ordinary or average, both of wages and profits and of rents. ... These ordinary or average

[1] See J. G. D. Clark, *Prehistoric Europe*, Chap. IX.
[2] *The Wealth of Nations*, Vol. I, pp. 44 and 42.

rates may be called the natural rates of wages, profit and rent, at the
time and place in which they commonly prevail. When the price of
any commodity is neither more nor less than is sufficient to pay
[these natural rates] the commodity is then sold for what may be
called its natural price. The commodity is then sold for precisely
what it is worth.[1]

As a theory of prices this is rather simple-minded, but it is
doubtful whether the doctrines taught nowadays, though so
much more elaborate, are any more penetrating. However
that may be, the point is not in the analysis; the point is in the
moral dilemma. Property and profits are an imposition upon
the workers. There is a note of nostalgia for "that original
state of affairs" when the worker had "neither landlord nor
master to share with him."[2]

But Adam Smith is being hard-headed. This book is devoted
not to moral sentiments but to expediency. The way lies ahead,
through the increasing productivity that follows the division
of labour. A sketchy theory of value will serve well enough,
for the main point is to argue the advantages of free trade and
accumulation of stock. The important thing is increasing
physical output, and prices do not really matter very much.

For Ricardo, also, value was a side issue. Ricardo did not
originally set out to look for a theory of prices —

The produce of the earth—all that is derived from its surface by
the united application of labour, machinery, and capital, is divided
among three classes of the community; namely, the proprietor of the
land, the owner of the stock or capital necessary for its cultivation, and
the labourers by whose industry it is cultivated.

But in different stages of society, the proportions of the whole
produce of the earth which will be allotted to each of these classes,
under the names of rent, profit, and wages, will be essentially
different; depending mainly on the actual fertility of the soil, on the

[1] Ibid., p. 48.
[2] Ibid., p. 57.

accumulation of capital and population, and on the skill, ingenuity, and instruments employed in agriculture.

To determine the laws which regulate this distribution, is the principal problem in Political Economy.[1]

But he was held up by the need to measure the total that was to be distributed. His difficulty was that a change in the share of wages in the value of output, which entails a change in the rate of profit on capital, alters the relative prices of commodities, because wages and profits enter in different proportions into the costs of each. In what unit should the product be valued? He made use of a unit of labour time, but he was never satisfied with it, and tinkered at it through various editions of the *Principles*, as Mr. Sraffa has shown. The point comes out most clearly in his last paper, which was found in the famous tin box at Raheny[2] —

The only qualities necessary to make a measure of value a perfect one are, that it should itself have value, and that that value should be itself invariable, in the same manner as in a perfect measure of length the measure should have length and that length should be neither liable to be increased nor diminished; or in a measure of weight that it should have weight and that such weight should be constant.

Although it is thus easy to say what a perfect measure of value should be it is not equally easy to find any one commodity that has the qualities required. When we want a measure of length we select a yard or a foot—which is some determined definite length neither liable to increase or diminish, but when we want a measure of value what commodity that has value are we to select which shall itself not vary in value?[3]

We can see clearly now that this is off the mark. Weight and length, of course, are human conventions, but once the con-

[1] *Works of David Ricardo*, ed. P. Sraffa, Vol. I, Preface to the *Principles*, p. 5.
[2] Ibid., Vol. I, p. ix.
[3] Ibid., Vol. IV, p. 361.

vention is established they do not change, for practical purposes, because they refer to the physical, non-human world. They are the same for Robinson Crusoe as in Trafalgar Square; the same in Moscow as in New York. But value is a relationship between people. It has no meaning at all for Robinson Crusoe. There never will be a unit for measuring national income that has the same meaning for everyone, still less a unit that means the same thing at different dates or in the setting of different economic systems.

We know now that when you cannot get an answer there is something wrong with the question, but Ricardo never saw that the mistake was in the question and he kept right on trying to eliminate mistakes in his answers.

There does not seem to be any ideological overtones or any smell of wishful thinking in Ricardo's pursuit of *absolute value*. He had a candour of mind which is sadly rare in those who concern themselves with social and political problems; he was honestly battling with an honest intellectual puzzle. But the argument was taken up in ideological terms and, until Mr. Sraffa rescued him, there was foisted upon him quite another question.

His labour-unit as a measure of *value* somehow seemed to lead to dangerous thoughts. Was labour alone to have the credit for creating *value*? Does this imply that profits are an imposition on the workers? The corrections that Ricardo made in his search for a unit of *value* were taken to show that he admitted that capital also is productive, and the whole argument sailed off into a fog of metaphysics masquerading as analysis.

Marshall took it upon himself to defend Ricardo against the imputation of dangerous thoughts. Misunderstandings have been due to obscurity —

His exposition is as confused as his thought is profound; he uses words in artificial senses, which he does not explain, and to which he does not adhere; and he changes from one hypothesis to another without giving notice.

If then we seek to understand him rightly, we must interpret him generously, more generously than he himself interpreted Adam Smith. When his words are ambiguous, we must give them that interpretation which other passages in his writings indicate that he would have wished to give them.[1]

So he fathers upon him "waiting" as an element in the cost of production. With the side heading "He corrects Malthus' anticipation of Marx's misunderstanding" he quotes Ricardo —

"Mr. Malthus appears to think that it is a part of my doctrine that the cost and value of a thing should be the same; it is, if he means by cost, 'cost of production' including profits. In the above passage, this is what he does not mean, and therefore he has not clearly understood me." And yet Rodbertus and Karl Marx claim Ricardo's authority for the statement that the natural value of things consists solely of the labour spent on them; and even those German economists who most strenuously combat the conclusions of these writers, are often found to admit that they have interpreted Ricardo rightly, and that their conclusions follow logically from his.[2]

The whole episode is a good example of the relations between analysis and ideology, all the more so since no one feels very keenly about it nowadays and we can view it with detachment.

Marshall was perfectly well aware that Ricardo was looking only for a measure of value. At the end of the appendix from which the above quotations are taken he writes —

Ricardo's first chapter has been discussed here with sole reference to the causes which govern the relative exchange values of different things; because its chief influence on subsequent thought has been in this direction. But it was originally associated with a controversy as to the extent to which the price of labour affords a good standard for measuring the general purchasing power of money.[3]

[1] Marshall, *Principles*, p. 813.
[2] Loc. cit., p. 816.
[3] Loc. cit., p. 821.

The shift in the argument, from a measure of *value* to a theory of the determination of relative prices, was connected with the shift in interest from Ricardo's problem — the laws which regulate the distribution of the produce of the earth between the classes of the community — to the much less burning topic of relative prices. But, under the surface, the problem of distribution was still supplying heat to this tepid question. The mysterious emanation, *value*, was still somehow lurking in relative prices, though they were now proclaimed to be merely the exchange rates between commodities; if labour alone was to be given credit for determining relative prices it somehow would get the credit for creating *value*, and, if labour created it, surely labour ought to have it? Adam Smith's hard-headed view, that the landlord and the master muscle in and take their share, will not do for a more pious generation. Capital must be allowed to create the value that it receives. And so it works round that the problem which bothered Ricardo in his search for a measure of *value* — the fact that the ratio of profits to wages, in the prices of different commodities, must vary with the ratio of capital to labour in producing them — is turned into a moral justification for profits, and an answer to the insidious view that labour ought to receive the *value* that it creates.

2

Marshall knew all the time what Ricardo had really meant, but he did not understand Marx. Marx's use of the labour theory of *value* was by no means the simple claim that the labourer has a right to the produce of his labour. On the contrary, his claim is that the theory of *value* is precisely what accounts for exploitation.

Like the others, he felt obliged to offer a theory of relative prices, but though he thought it essential we can see that it is irrelevant to the main point of his argument.

In Vol. I of *Capital* he deals with relative prices in the famous passage —

Let us take two commodities, e.g. corn and iron. The proportions in which they are exchangeable, whatever those proportions may be, can always be represented by an equation in which a given quantity of corn is equated to some quantity of iron: e.g. 1 quarter corn = $x$ cwt iron. What does this equation tell us? It tells us that in two different things — in 1 quarter of corn and $x$ cwt of iron, there exists in equal quantities something common to both. The two things must therefore be equal to a third, which in itself is neither the one nor the other. Each of them, so far as it is exchange value, must therefore be reducible to this third.

This common "something" cannot be either a geometrical, a chemical, or any other natural property of commodities. Such properties claim our attention only in so far as they affect the utility of those commodities, make them use-values. But the exchange of commodities is evidently an act characterized by a total abstraction from use-value.

If we then leave out of consideration the use-value of commodities, they have only one common property left, that of being products of labour. But even the product of labour itself has undergone a change in our hands. If we make abstraction from its use-value, we make abstraction at the same time from the material elements and shapes that make the product a use-value; we see in it no longer a table, a house, yarn, or any other useful thing. Its existence as a material thing is put out of sight. Neither can it any longer be regarded as the product of the labour of the joiner, the mason, the spinner, or of any other definite kind of productive labour. Along with the useful qualities of the products themselves, we put out of sight both the useful character of the various kinds of labour embodied in them, and the concrete forms of that labour; there is nothing left but what is common to them all; all are reduced to one and the same sort of labour, human labour in the abstract. ...

All that these things now tell us is, that human labour-power has been expended in their production, that human labour is embodied in them. When looked at as crystals of this social substance, common to them all, they are — Values.[1]

Gerald Shove, objecting to the present writer describing this as "a purely dogmatic statement" maintains that it is an argument.[2] But it is hard to see any argument in it. Here *value* is something different from price, which accounts for price, and which in turn has to be accounted for. And to account for it by labour-time is mere assertion. If we define *value* as the labour-time required to produce a commodity, and then advance the proposition that commodities normally exchange at prices proportional to their *values* in this sense, then we have reduced it from a metaphysical statement to a hypothesis. But it is a hypothesis that it would be a waste of time to test, for we know in advance, and Marx also knows, that it is not accurate.

This theory of prices is not a myth, like Adam Smith's tale of the beavers and deer. Nor was it intended to be an original contribution to science. It was simply an orthodox dogma. The conflation of the idea of labour as the measure of *value* and labour as the cause of *value* was taken over from Ricardo, and as we see from Ricardo's last work, which Marx never read, it was not a misunderstanding; it was very close to the way Ricardo saw it himself.

The point of the argument was something quite different. Accepting the dogma that all things exchange at prices proportional to their *values*, Marx applies it to labour power. This is the clue that explains capitalism. The worker receives his *value*, his cost in terms of labour-time, and the employer makes use of him to produce more *value* than he costs. The cost of the worker is a subsistence wage. (This is not a bare physiological minimum but contains a "historical and moral element" depending on the standard of life at the time when "the class of free labour is formed."[3])

[1] *Capital*, Vol. I, pp. 3-5.
[2] "Mrs. Robinson on Marxian Economics," *Economic Journal*, April 1944.
[3] *Capital*, Vol. I, p. 150.

Marx does not indict capitalism in the manner of the naïve idealists who treat exploitation as robbery. On the contrary, with a kind of logical sarcasm, he defends capitalism. There is no swindle — everything exchanges for its *value*, as is right and just. It is not the *value* he produces, but the *value* that he costs which is the worker's due.

On this plane the whole argument appears to be metaphysical; it provides a typical example of the way metaphysical ideas operate. Logically it is a mere rigmarole of words but for Marx it was a flood of illumination and for latter-day Marxists, a source of inspiration.

Ideologically, it is much stronger poison than a direct attack on injustice. The system is not unjust within its own rules. For that very reason reform is impossible; there is nothing for it but to overthrow the system itself.

On the scientific plane, it offers the basis for an approach to the analysis of capitalism.

Marx had learned from Ricardo the trick of setting up what we now call a model — stating the assumptions and drawing the conclusions. He backed up his dogma about the *value* of labour-power with an analytical argument.

Capitalism first recruits the workers that it needs by ruining the peasant and the artisan. The standard of life that prevails when "the class of free labour is formed" sets the level for real-wage rates. The surplus of production over wages belongs to the capitalists. This is no metaphysical surplus of *value*; it is a concrete surplus of goods, in particular of wage-goods. The capitalists use the surplus drawn from the output on one set of workers to employ others — some to supply their own wants and those of their hangers-on; and some, the greater part, to build up more capital to extract more surplus. The labour-force is increasing all the time (an obvious assumption to make at that period) and there is a reserve army of potential workers un-employed. This provides a mechanism which prevents real

wages from rising permanently above the level at which they
started. When capital has been accumulating so fast as to run
the reserve of labour low, the level of real wages rises and the
surplus per man employed falls. Accumulation slows up. (Here
there is a weak point in Marx's argument, for a trade-cycle
theory of a failure in the inducement to invest when future
expected profits seem low gets mixed up with the reduced flow
of resources when past realized profits are low.) Not only does
the reduction in profits slow down accumulation, so that the
supply of labour runs ahead, but also the high wages induce
labour-saving devices to be introduced. Natural growth, ahead
of the now slow pace of accumulation, together with technological unemployment, replenish the reserve army and real
wages are brought down again.

Here the metaphysical theory has been transformed into a
scientific hypothesis — the hypothesis that under capitalism
real-wage rates do not rise. It seemed very plausible at the time,
but it has turned out to be wrong. This, indeed, is the proof of
its scientific status. A metaphysical belief, as in the *law of value*,
cannot be wrong and this is the sign that there is nothing to be
learned from it.

For obvious reasons it was the dogmatic rather than the
scientific element in Marxism that supported a great historic
movement and blossomed into an orthodox ideology. The
scientific element atrophied, for science progresses by trial and
error, and when it is forbidden to admit error there can be no
progress. Even to this day Marxists prefer to deny that capitalism has raised the standard of life of the workers, or else to deny
that Marx predicted that it would not, choosing to sacrifice the
scientific element in the development of his thought in order
to prop up the dogmatic element.

The anti-Marxists were no better: in their attacks upon him
they also concentrated on the metaphysics; in particular they

fastened upon the theory of relative prices as the easiest point at which to score hits.

Marx elaborated his theory of relative prices so that it came out quite differently from the simple dogma of Vol. I of *Capital*. Loyal Marxists very much resent the suggestion that there is any inconsistency between the versions in Vol. I and Vol. III, and as far as Marx himself is concerned it is fairer to regard it as a modification rather than an inconsistency. In Vol. I he says that the normal prices of commodities are proportional to their *values*, and in Vol. III that this is so only for commodities which happen to require the overall average ratio of capital per man employed (translating into academic terminology). In any case Marx never succeeded in getting the rest of his ideas into a coherent, integrated form, like Vol. I, and he did not publish them. No one can fairly be accused of inconsistency in un-finished work. It was Engels who announced that the third volume would contain a reconciliation of the Law of Value with the equality of the rate of profit in lines of production with different ratios of capital and labour. He made a great thing of it, and opened what Böhm-Bawerk mockingly called a prize-essay competition for suggested solutions.[1] When at last Vol. III appeared, there was no solution at all, but only, dressed up in a rigmarole, the commonplace that prices cover costs of produc-tion including normal profits on the capital concerned.

Böhm-Bawerk was delighted to be able to exercise his wit at Marx's expense, and academic economists ever since have been much relieved to be able to tell their pupils that Marx's system is founded on a simple confusion. The Marxists more-over have rallied to the defence with exceedingly far-fetched arguments. But Marx's theory did not in any essential depend on all this, one way or the other. The essence of his theory, in its metaphysical aspect, concerned the *value* of labour power;

[1] *Karl Marx and the Close of his System*. (This English title is a mistranslation. Böhm meant the completion of the analysis.)

in its scientific aspect, the share of wages in the product of industry; this was completely untouched either by Böhm's merry quips or his own defenders' turgid replies.

The whole thing, considered analytically, was a great fuss about nothing. For the analysis of *relative* prices we really cannot do any better than Adam Smith's simple-minded theory.[1] The general development of an economy determines the general level of wages, interest, profit and rent (it is here that all the most interesting questions lie). For each particular commodity the normal price is governed by its normal costs of production on this basis (exception made, as Adam Smith is careful to do, for monopoly and natural scarcities), because each industry must be able to pay its factors of production at more or less the same rate as all the rest.

So far as the general run of manufacturing industries is concerned (at least up till now — automation may bring a change of emphasis) the predominant element determining differences in cost is output per man hour of labour employed. The difference in price between a tea-cup and a motor-car, or even between an Austin and a Rolls Royce, is mainly to be accounted for by differences in the wage bill incurred in producing a unit of each. (It is this "wages theory of value," projected back into primitive conditions, which gave rise to Adam Smith's mythical labour theory of value.)

It is not true of natural commodities (though Marx would never admit it). The difference in price between a ton of platinum and a ton of lead is much greater than the inverse of the differences in output per head; so is the difference in price of a pound of vintage grapes and a pound of gooseberries.

But for manufacturing industry, surely, everyone would agree that, on the one hand, differences in prices are more or less proportional to labour cost, and on the other hand they are not exactly proportional, because of differences in the grades

1 Cf. above, p. 30.

of labour employed, in capital per man and in the scale at which investment has to be made.

What is all the fuss about? Does not any reasonable theory of relative prices come to much the same thing? Certainly it does if it is reasonable; the dispute was not, is not, on the plane of reason. It is the ideological overtones that cause all the trouble.

No one, of course, is conscious of his own ideology, any more than he can smell his own breath. Marx in particular felt himself to be perfectly scientific and strongly disapproved of the kind of idealistic socialism that depends upon moral sentiment. His analysis showed capitalism as a necessary stage in economic development, required to ripen the productive power of social labour, which cannot and must not be overthrown before it has fulfilled its historic mission. Meanwhile the capitalists are quite as much the servants of the system as anyone else. Schumpeter's innovating entrepreneur, the benefactor of mankind, is the same character as Marx's Moneybags. Only the adjectives are different. For Marx, of course, hated their guts. Every word he wrote is saturated in moral indignation and Marxism, in its original form (like Christianity), had the appeal of the cause of the under-dog. As with Christianity, the wheel of time has brought it to be a creed for top dogs and its moral appeal has been much weakened thereby.

3

What about practical applications of theory? How does the *law of value*, which was devised to penetrate the disguises of capitalism, turn out in a socialist economy?

First of all, labour-value as a unit of measurement of National Income is quite useless. We cannot estimate the total *value* of the goods produced in a year by simply totting up the hours of labour that have gone into them.

To begin with there is the problem of distinguishing between productive and unproductive labour. This goes back to Adam Smith —

There is one sort of labour which adds to the value of the subject upon which it is bestowed; there is another which has no such effect. The former, as it produces a value, may be called productive, the latter, unproductive labour. Thus the labour of a manufacturer adds generally to the value of the materials which he works upon, that of his own maintenance, and of his master's profit. The labour of a menial servant, on the contrary, adds to the value of nothing. Though the manufacturer has his wages advanced to him by his master, he in reality costs him no expense, the value of those wages being generally restored, together with a profit, in the improved value of the subject upon which his labour is bestowed. But the maintenance of a menial servant never is restored.

The labour of some of the most respectable orders in the society is, like that of menial servants, unproductive of any value, and does not fix or realize itself in any permanent subject, or vendible commodity, which endures after that labour is past, and for which an equal quantity of labour could afterwards be procured. The sovereign, for example, with all the officers both of justice and war who serve under him, the whole army and navy, are unproductive labourers. They are the servants of the public, and are maintained by a part of the annual produce of the industry of other people. Their service, how honourable, how useful, or how necessary soever, produces nothing for which an equal quantity of service can afterwards be procured. The protection, security, and defence, of the commonwealth, the effect of their labour this year, will not purchase its protection, security, and defence, for the year to come. In the same class must be ranked, some both of the gravest and most important, and some of the most frivolous professions; churchmen, lawyers, physicians, men of letters of all kinds; players, buffoons, musicians, opera-singers, opera dancers, etc. The labour of the meanest of these has a certain value, regulated by the very same principles which regulate that of every other sort of labour; and that of the noblest and most useful produces nothing which could afterwards purchase or procure an equal quantity of labour. Like the declamation of the actor, the harangue of the orator, or the tune of the musician, the work of all of them perishes in the very instant of its production.[1]

Adam Smith is groping for the concept of labour which contributes to the process of accumulation. Marx took over the distinction between productive and unproductive labour. He includes transport as productive, but excludes commerce. In practice, in calculating National Income in the socialist countries, the line seems to be drawn between physical commodities and services. Thus a hat is part of National Income, but a hair-do is not. There may be very good empirical reasons for this procedure. A growth of productivity can be measured much more easily when there is a physical output (though differences in quality are hard to catch), while services can only be valued at what they cost. But from a philosophical point of view the distinction between *value*-producing labour and the rest is not very easy to understand.

The second difficulty concerns the quality of workers. How can we find out how much *abstract labour* is contained in an hour's work of a skilled engineer? To use the relative wages of different grades of workers to assess the different amounts of *value* they contribute to a product is not legitimate; differences in wages are supposed to measure differences in the *values* of labour-power, that is the cost of supporting and training the workers, not differences in *value* created.

The next difficulty is that *value* is the product not of the hours of work actually expended on a job, but of socially necessary labour time. Marx was careful to avoid the absurd argument that the products of a slow worker contain more *value* than the product of an efficient one. Technical progress and accumulation of capital equipment reduce the *value* of given commodities, and when obsolete methods are still being used side by side with superior techniques or when some groups of workers are using

[1] *Wealth of Nations*, Vol. I, p. 294.

more mechanical equipment than others, and at the same time some are more efficient than others within each group, how can we work out the exact figure for the *socially necessary labour time* for each branch of production?

Finally, the *value* of a year's production is not only the labour expended during the year, but also the *value* given up by the capital goods in which labour time was embodied in the past. This brings into the argument all the notoriously perplexing questions concerned with depreciation of plant and valuation of stocks.

But if all these difficulties could somehow or other be overcome, the *value* unit would still be otiose, for it does not measure what the measurers are interested in. Productivity and the growth of National Income are conceived as flows of outputs of goods; it is precisely the changes in physical output per man hour that have to be watched. In terms of *value*, an hour is an hour. A constant quantity of labour-time, year after year, produces the same *value*. But who cares? What we want to know is how much *stuff* it is producing.

In practice the socialist economists have to tot up their National Incomes in money terms, and they have just the same problems about index numbers, the same puzzles about historic *versus* replacement cost, the same temptation to make figures mean more than they can, as their capitalist colleagues. The theory of *value* does not help them in the least.

As a theory of real wages the *value* of labour power clearly has no place in a socialist economy. The plan which regulates production is not aiming at extracting a surplus for its own sake but at taking whatever is needed to finance investment, defence, social services and the general overheads of society. A Keynesian theory of real wages is the appropriate one, the relation of prices to money wages being governed by the ratio of investment to consumption.

At the same time the socialist economy is proud to show a

faster rate of accumulation than any capitalist economy has ever done. To have labelled investable resources "exploitation" and "unpaid labour" is somewhat embarrassing. To argue that the capitalists extract surplus for their own benefit while the social planners are concerned with the good of society is to argue on the subjective, moral plane; objectively considered, the capitalists in Marx's scheme were an organ of society whose function was to secure accumulation, just like the socialist planners. As Keynes puts it: "Like bees they saved and accumulated, not less to the advantage of the whole community because they themselves held narrower ends in prospect."[1] As we see nowadays in South-East Asia or the Caribbean, the misery of being exploited by capitalists is nothing compared to the misery of not being exploited at all. Here the *law of value* develops a kind of squint that leaves one deeply confused.

What about relative prices? To make the prices of commodities sold in the shops proportional to their *values* would entail collecting the fund for investment, etc., by a uniform tax on the wages bill and allowing prices to cover costs including the tax. There is a lot to recommend such a system, though it would have to be modified to bring prices into line with the conditions of supply and demand, for *values* would correspond to demand prices only when all particular scarcities had been overcome so that each commodity individually was in perfectly elastic supply. No such system of pricing has been attempted, and there does not seem to be any clear doctrine concerning relative prices in socialist theory. The textbook of *Political Economy* only tells us that "the operation of the law of value is taken into account in the planning of prices"[2]; it does not say how.

The textbook lays great stress on the distinction between the two kinds of production which exist in the Soviet Union —

[1] *Economic Consequences of the Peace*, p. 16.
[2] Op. cit., p. 591.

fully socialist production in industry, where the whole of the means of production is owned by the State and workers receive wages; and co-operative production in most of agriculture, where the major part of the means of production is owned by the co-operative and the workers receive a share in the produce.

How is it possible to derive the prices of agricultural commodities from their *values*? This has never been explained. Within a collective farm, presumably, the correct procedure is to evaluate various jobs so that a labour-day is about as hard to earn in one as in another. But the money return for a labour-day to the farm as a whole depends upon the prices that it receives for its produce; these are partly fixed by the authorities and partly subject to the vagaries of supply and demand in the free market. Is it *value* that determines prices or prices that determine *values*?

Among all the various meanings of *value*, there has been one all the time under the surface, the old concept of a Just Price — the principle that made Adam Smith's hunters swap their game on the basis of the time that each species usually took to catch. It is this meaning that is wanted here. Prices ought to be such (subject to political expediency) that a day's work in the country and in the town brings in about the same income. But even when this is granted as an ideal there still remains the problem of calculating what is to be considered an equivalent income for individuals leading quite different kinds of life in different environments. *Value* will not help. It has no operational content. It is just a word.

# III

## THE NEO-CLASSICS: UTILITY

MEANWHILE, from the orthodox camp the labour theory, with its disagreeable smell, had been swept out and *utility* had come in.

I

*Utility* is a metaphysical concept of impregnable circularity; *utility* is the quality in commodities that makes individuals want to buy them, and the fact that individuals want to buy commodities shows that they have *utility*.

It came into vogue first in connexion with the theory of relative prices. Purporting to be a quantity, it could be spoken of in terms of total, average and marginal, and so used to explain the old puzzle of water and diamonds. The total *utility* of water is indefinitely great, since life itself depends on it. When individuals have all they need they are not willing to pay for any more. In Aden, however, where water is scarce, it commands a price and the quantity that an individual consumes is cut back to the amount whose *marginal utility* is equal to the price. How do we know? It must be so, for price is the measure of *marginal utility*.

It was this idea that came to Jevons with the force of illumination. "In the past few months I have fortunately struck out what I have no doubt is the true *Theory of Economy*, so thorough going and consistent, that I cannot now read other books on the subject without indignation."[1]

Marshall had discovered it independently in connexion with the idea of consumer's surplus.[2] By the time it appears in the

[1] *Letters and Journals*, p. 151.
[2] *Pure Theory of Domestic Values.*

47

final version of his *Principles of Economics* he has hedged it round with many qualifications —

Utility is taken to be correlative to Desire or Want. It has been already argued that desires cannot be measured directly, but only indirectly by the outward phenomena to which they give rise: and that in those cases with which economics is chiefly concerned the measure is found in the price which a person is willing to pay for the fulfilment or satisfaction of his desire. He may have desires and aspirations which are not consciously set for any satisfaction: but for the present we are concerned chiefly with those which do so aim; and we assume that the resulting satisfaction corresponds in general fairly well to that which was anticipated when the purchase was made.

There is an endless variety of wants, but there is a limit to each separate want. This familiar and fundamental tendency of human nature may be stated in the *law of satiable wants* or *of diminishing utility* thus: The *total utility* of a thing to anyone (that is, the total pleasure or other benefit it yields him) increases with every increase in his stock of it, but not as fast as his stock increases. If his stock of it increases at a uniform rate the benefit derived from it increases at a diminishing rate. In other words, the additional benefit which a person derives from a given increase of his stock of a thing, diminishes with every increase in the stock that he already has. ...

It cannot be too much insisted that to measure directly, or *per se*, either desires or the satisfaction which results from their fulfilment is impossible, if not inconceivable. If we could, we should have two accounts to make up, one of desires, and the other of realized satisfactions. And the two might differ considerably. For, to say nothing of higher aspirations, some of those desires with which economics is chiefly concerned, and especially those connected with emulation, are impulsive; many result from the force of habit; some are morbid and lead only to hurt; and many are based on expectations that are never fulfilled. ... Of course many satisfactions are not common pleasures, but belong to the development of a man's higher nature, or to use a good old word, to his *beatification*; and some may even partly result from self-abnegation. ... The two direct measurements then might differ. But as neither of them is possible, we fall back on the measurement which economics supplies, of the motive or moving force to action: and we make it serve, with all its faults, *both* for the desires which prompt activities and for the satisfactions that result from them.[1]

It is the desire, not the satisfaction, that is measured by price, yet the idea of satisfaction cannot be kept out. *Utility* is a Good Thing; the aim and purpose of economic life is to get as much of it as possible. And, set out in a diagram, it looks just like a measurable quantity.

Before going any further, we must sadly observe that all the modern refinements of this concept have not freed it from metaphysics. We are told nowadays that since *utility* cannot be measured it is not an operational concept, and that "revealed preference" should be put in its place. Observable market behaviour will show what an individual chooses. Preference is just what the individual under discussion prefers; there is no value judgment involved. Yet, as the argument goes on, it is clear that it is a Good Thing for the individual to have what he prefers. This, it may be held, is not a question of satisfaction, but freedom — we want him to have what he prefers so as to avoid having to restrain his behaviour.

But drug-fiends should be cured; children should go to school. How do we decide what preferences should be respected and what restrained unless we judge the preferences themselves?

It is quite impossible for us to do that violence to our own natures to refrain from value judgments.

Moreover, it is just not true that market behaviour can reveal preferences. It is not only that the experiment of offering an individual alternative bundles of goods, or changing his income just to see what he will buy, could never be carried out in practice. The objection is logical, not only practical.

As Marshall says —

There is however an implicit condition in this law [the law of diminishing marginal utility] which should be made clear. It is that

---

[1] *Principles*, pp. 92–3.

we do not suppose time to be allowed for any alteration in the character or tastes of the man himself. It is therefore no exception to the law that the more good music a man hears, the stronger is his taste for it likely to become; that avarice and ambition are often insatiable; or that the virtue of cleanliness and the vice of drunkenness alike grow on what they feed upon. For in such cases our observations range over some period of time; and the man is not the same at the beginning as at the end of it. If we take a man as he is, without allowing time for any change in his character, the marginal utility of a thing to him diminishes steadily with every increase in his supply of it.[1]

We can observe the reaction of an individual to two different sets of prices only at two different times. How can we tell what part of the difference in his purchases is due to the difference in prices and what part to the change in his preferences that has taken place meanwhile? There is certainly no presumption that his character has *not* changed, for soap and whisky are not the only goods whose use affects tastes. Practically everything develops either an inertia of habit or a desire for change.

We have got one equation for two unknowns. Unless we can get some independent evidence about preferences the experiment is no good. But it was the experiment that we were supposed to rely on to observe the preferences.

This is not the only difficulty. For Jevons, and in his less cautious moments for Marshall, the consumer is "a man," a Robinson Crusoe, an individual with his tight, impermeable, insulated equipment of desires and tastes. When we admit the influence of society, of the Joneses, of advertisement, upon the individual's scale of preferences, the problem of framing the experiment becomes teasing indeed. Worse still, when we recognize that one man's consumption may reduce the welfare of others — a consideration which the existence of each other's motor-cars forces painfully upon us — we begin to doubt whether preferences are what we really prefer.

[1] *Principles*, p. 94.

Let us leave this logic-chopping and return to *utility* — a metaphysical concept, a mere word, that has no scientific content, yet one which expresses a point of view.

The ideological content of the *utility* approach to prices was curiously double-edged, as Gunnar Myrdal has pointed out.[1]

From one angle it was far more humane than the classical theory. For the first time, wages were included in the wealth of the nation. Adam Smith rather liked to think of workers enjoying "affluence," but basically wages were a cost for him and a nation that has attained the highest degree of opulence would be one in which labour was cheap.[2] For Ricardo also wealth meant accumulation. For the neo-classicals the *utility* of goods consumed by workers was no different from any other.

Wicksell was clear on this point —

As soon as we begin seriously to regard economic phenomena *as a whole* and to seek for the conditions of the welfare of the whole, consideration for the interests of the proletariat must emerge; and from thence to the proclamation of *equal* rights for all is only a short step.

The very concept of political economy, therefore, or the existence of a science with such a name implies, strictly speaking, a thoroughly revolutionary programme. It is not surprising that the concept is vague, for that often happens with a revolutionary programme. Indeed, many practical and theoretical problems remain to be solved before the goal of economic or social development can be said to be clearly understood. Something can still be said in favour of the older point of view, but in any case it should be said straightforwardly and without prevarication. If, for example, we regard the working classes as beings of a lower type, or if, without going so far as this, we regard them as not yet being ready for a full share in the product of society, then we should say so clearly and base our further reasoning upon that

[1] Lectures delivered at Cambridge in 1950. See also *The Political Element in the Development of Economic Theory*.

[2] *Wealth of Nations*, Vol. I, p. 84.

opinion. There is only one thing which is unworthy of science — to conceal or pervert the truth; that is to say, in this case, to represent the position as if those classes had already received all they could reasonably wish or expect, or to rely upon unfounded, optimistic beliefs that economic developments in themselves tend to the greatest possible satisfaction of all.[1]

Not only that, but the doctrine of diminishing marginal utility applied to income itself. As Marshall put it —

A stronger incentive will be required to induce a person to pay a given price for anything if he is poor than if he is rich. A shilling is the measure of less pleasure, or satisfaction of any kind, to a rich man than to a poor one. A rich man in doubt whether to spend a shilling on a single cigar, is weighing against one another smaller pleasures than a poor man, who is doubting whether to spend a shilling on a supply of tobacco that will last him a month. The clerk with £100 a year will walk to business in a much heavier rain than the clerk with £300 a year; for the cost of a ride by tram or omnibus measures a greater benefit to the poorer man than to the richer. If the poorer man spends the money, he will suffer more from the want of it afterwards than the richer would. The benefit that is measured in the poorer man's mind by the cost is greater than that measured by it in the richer man's mind.[2]

This points to egalitarian principles, justifies Trade Unions, progressive taxation and the Welfare State, if not more radical means to interfere with an economic system that allows so much of the good juice of *utility* to evaporate out of commodities by distributing them unequally.

But on the other hand the whole point of *utility* was to justify *laisser faire*. Everyone must be free to spend his income as he likes, and he will gain the greatest benefit when he equalizes the *marginal utility* of a shilling spent on each kind of good. The pursuit of profit, under conditions of perfect

[1] *Lectures on Political Economy*, Vol. I, p. 4.
[2] *Principles*, p. 19.

competition, leads producers to equate marginal costs to prices, and the maximum possible satisfaction is drawn from available resources.

This is an ideology to end ideologies, for it has abolished the moral problem. It is only necessary for each individual to act egoistically for the good of all to be attained.

This conception, indeed, goes back to Adam Smith (perhaps to Adam). The central thesis of the *Wealth of Nations* is —

The natural effort which every man is continually making to better his own condition, is a principle of preservation capable of preventing and correcting, in many respects, the bad effects of a political economy, in some degree both partial and oppressive. Such a political economy, though it no doubt retards more or less, is not always capable of stopping altogether the natural progress of a nation towards wealth and prosperity.[1]

In another passage —

It is not from the benevolence of the butcher, the brewer or the baker, that we expect our dinner, but from their regard to their own interest. We address ourselves, not to their humanity, but to their self-love, and never talk to them of our own necessities, but of their advantages. Nobody but a beggar chooses to depend chiefly upon the benevolence of his fellow-citizens.[2]

Adam Smith does not find the "natural propensity in human nature ... to truck, barter and exchange one thing for another"[3] particularly admirable; a note of gentlemanly distaste often comes into his tone — but there it is; this is the foundation of national prosperity and it has only to be freed from restraint to blossom in full perfection. (Perhaps it was because he could not really answer him that Mandeville got under his skin.)

By the neo-classicals this was carried to extremes, and there

[1] *Wealth of Nations*, Vol. II, p. 168.
[2] Ibid., Vol. I, p. 13.
[3] Ibid., p. 12.

have been some who even deny that it is necessary for authority to decide whether traffic should keep to the right or the left.

So pure a faith, of course, is rare; most writers had doubts at one point or another. Walras believed himself to be a socialist, and Marshall in his young days had a tendency in that direction. It was the writings of the socialists that repelled him.[1]

Wicksell saw through the whole thing. Walras, he observes, set out to provide a rigorous proof of the vague doctrine of the classics.

It is necessary to prove that free competition provides the maximum of utility. And this view was in fact the starting point of his own work in economics. It is almost tragic, however, that Walras, who was usually so acute and clear-headed, imagined that he had found the rigorous proof, which he missed in the contemporary defenders of the free trade dogma, merely because he clothed in a mathematical formula the very arguments which he considered insufficient when they were expressed in ordinary language.[2]

Pigou's distinction between private and social net products opened a wide breach through which exceptions could flock in.

The general emphasis, all the same, was heavily on the side of laisser faire.

How was it possible to keep the two sides of the doctrine apart — the thoroughly revolutionary programme indicated by utility theory and the thoroughly conservative ideology of laisser faire ?

First of all we must realize that, although logically the task presents insuperable difficulties, on the theological plane it was really quite easy. The pupils of the economists, though not owners of great possessions, yet on the whole belonged to strata in society that did not lose by inequality. Those with socialist leanings generally rejected the whole subject as an imposture anyway. The students of the subject were quite ready to have their social consciences soothed.

The method by which the egalitarian element in the doctrine was sterilized was mainly by slipping from *utility* to physical output as the object to be maximized. A smaller total of physical goods, equally distributed, admittedly may yield more *utility* than a much larger total unequally distributed, but if we keep our eye on the total of goods it is easy to forget about the *utility*. Marshall cured himself of his socialist leanings by considering the physical national income.

I developed a tendency to socialism; which was fortified later on by Mill's essay in the *Fortnightly Review* in 1879. Thus for more than a decade, I remained under the conviction that the suggestions, which are associated with the word "socialism," were the most important subject of study, if not in the world, yet at all events for me. But the writings of socialists generally repelled me, almost as much as they attracted me; because they seemed far out of touch with realities: and, partly for that reason, I decided to say little on the matter, till I had thought much longer.

Now, when old age indicates that my time for thought and speech is nearly ended, I see on all sides marvellous developments of working class faculty: and, partly in consequence, a broader and firmer foundation for socialistic schemes than existed when Mill wrote. But no socialistic scheme, yet advanced, seems to make adequate provision for the maintenance of high enterprise, and individual strength of character; nor to promise a sufficiently rapid increase in the business plant and other material implements of production to enable the real incomes of the manual labour classes to continue to increase as fast as they have done in the recent past, even if the total income of the country be shared equally by all.[1] ...

The average level of human nature in the western world has risen fast during the last fifty years. But it has seemed to me that those have made most real progress towards the distant goal of ideally perfect

[1] *Industry and Trade*, p. vii.

social organization, who have concentrated their energies on some
particular difficulties in the way, and not spent strength on endeavour-
ing to rush past them.[1]

In this mellow sunset of his life he felt able to reiterate what
he had written more than twenty years earlier —

The problem of social aims takes on new forms in every age: but
underlying all there is the one fundamental principle, viz. that
progress mainly depends on the extent to which the strongest, and
not merely the highest, forces of human nature can be utilized for the
increase of social good. There are some doubts as to what social good
really is; but they do not reach far enough to impair the foundations
of this fundamental principle. For there has always been a substratum
of agreement that social good lies mainly in that healthful exercise
and development of faculties which yields happiness without pall,
because it sustains self-respect and is sustained by hope. No utilization
of waste gases in the blast furnace can compare with the triumph of
making work for the public good pleasurable in itself, and of
stimulating men of all classes to great endeavours by other means
than that evidence of power which manifests itself by lavish expenditure. We need to foster fine work and fresh initiative by the warming
breath of the sympathy and appreciation of those who truly understand it; we need to turn consumption into paths that strengthen the
consumer and call forth the best qualities of those who provide for
consumption. Recognizing that some work must be done that is not
ennobling, we must seek to apply the growing knowledge and
material resources of the world to reduce such work within narrow
limits, and to extirpate all conditions of life which are in themselves
debasing. There cannot be a great sudden improvement in man's
conditions of life; for he forms them as much as they form him, and he
himself cannot change fast: but he must press on steadfastly towards
the distant goal where the opportunities of a noble life may be
accessible to all.[2]

Connected with this conception was the justification for

---

[1] Ibid., p. 664.
[2] Ibid., pp. 664, 665.

THE NEO-CLASSICS: UTILITY

inequality on the ground that only the rich save, so that inequality is necessary for capital accumulation. This savours somewhat of classical hard-headedness, but it was always presented in a mollified form — inequality could be relied upon to raise the total to be shared so much that even the smallest share would be larger than it could be in an egalitarian system. And as a subsidiary argument, we used to be taught that the redistribution of income would not really appreciably raise anyone's income at all.

There may have been a great deal of hard-headed sense in all this. The only point that concerns us here is the elegant conjuring trick by which the egalitarian moral of the *utility* theory was made to vanish before our eyes.

The other way of evading the egalitarian moral of *utility* theory was frankly to admit it but to separate it sharply from the question of the total to be distributed. Exercises are still set out in which it is assumed that distribution has been dealt with, for instance by a system of taxes and bounties, and then shown how a free market leads to maximum satisfaction. No one, of course, ever takes the taxes and bounties seriously, or inquires how an economic system depending on the money motive would work if income was doled out to individuals independently of their efforts; or how the profit motive could be made to operate when no one was allowed to keep what he acquired, above the average level, for the benefit of his own family.

In all this kind of analysis, which is still taught and is still being elaborated with fresh embellishments, the notion of ethical judgment purports to be excluded and the whole exercise is put forward as a piece of pure logic. The very idea of moral implications is abhorrent to practitioners in this field.

All the same, even economists are human beings, and cannot divest themselves of human habits of thought. Their system is saturated with moral feeling. Those within it, who have grown used to breathing its balmy air, have lost the power to smell it. To those approaching from outside who complain that the scent is sickly, the insiders indignantly reply: "The smell is in your own noses. Our aim is completely odourless, scientific, logical and free from value judgments."

The unconscious preoccupation behind the neo-classical system was chiefly to raise profits to the same level of moral respectability as wages. The labourer is worthy of his hire. What is the capitalist worthy of? The hard-headed attitude of the Classics, which recognized exploitation as the source of national wealth, was abandoned. Capital was no longer primarily an advance of wages made necessary by the fact that the worker has no property and cannot keep himself till the fruits of his labour appear. Capital is somehow identified with the time of waiting, and it produces the extra output that a longer gestation period makes possible. Since capital is productive, the capitalist has a right to his portion. Since only the rich save, inequality is justified. Meanwhile, the current of the thoroughly revolutionary programme flows aside to turn the idle wheels of the pure theory of Welfare.

2

There were two quite separate branches of the neo-classical system, each with its own analytical model and each with its own brand of anodyne for moral doubts.

The distinction is not much emphasized nowadays and is often completely overlooked. For instance, Schumpeter in the notes for his great *History of Economic Analysis* maintains that the hard core of Marshall's theory is much the same as the scheme set out by Walras.[1]

In fact there is a basic difference between them concerning

[1] Op. cit., p. 837.

the supply of capital. To Walras, to Jevons, the Austrians, Wicksell (and, perhaps, to Lord Robbins, who saw the allocation of scarce means between alternative uses as the central, if not sole, subject-matter of economics), it came naturally to take the supply of factors of production as given. Each employer of factors seeks to minimize the cost of his product and to maximize his own return, each particle of a factor seeks the employment that maximizes its income and each consumer plans his consumption to maximize *utility*. There is one equilibrium position in which each individual is doing the best for himself, so that no one has any incentive to move. (For groups to combine to better themselves collectively is strictly against the rules.) In this position each individual is receiving an income governed by the marginal productivity of the type of factor that he provides, and marginal productivity is governed by scarcity relatively to demand. Here "capital" is a factor like all the rest, and the distinction between work and property has disappeared from view. Setting the whole thing out in algebra is a great help. The symmetrical relations between $x$ and $y$ seem smooth and amiable, entirely free from the associations of acrimony which are apt to be suggested by the relations between "capital and labour"; and the apparent rationality of the system of distribution of the product between the factors of production conceals the arbitrary nature of the distribution of the factors between the chaps.

Marshall's scheme is quite different. The factors of production are not simply given, they have a supply price; there is a certain rate of return which it is necessary for a factor to receive to call a certain quantity of it into use. This price is not a cost, but it measures cost — the cost of the efforts and sacrifices of the workers and the capitalists. The efforts of the workers, of course, just means work. The sacrifice of the capitalists is *waiting*. This leaves land without a real cost and rent without a moral justification (but it is too late now to nationalize the land and, anyway, an individual capitalist who happens to have invested in real estate is *waiting* as much as anyone else).

Neither scheme ever succeeded in getting itself satisfactorily set out. The contradictions in each could pass unnoticed (or could be dismissed as puzzles to which there must be an answer that will soon be found) because the whole emphasis was not upon the structure of the system but upon its internal working — the theory of relative prices — which had now become the almost exclusive subject of discussion and was elaborated with endless detail.

The flaw in the first scheme is that it provides no way of accounting for a rate of profit on capital and a rate of interest on finance. The factors that are given are given in some concrete form: capital consists of machines and stocks of goods. In the market equilibrium, each machine has its own hire-price, derived from the demand for the particular commodities that it assists to produce. If there is any tendency to equalize the rate of profit on capital in general it must be because capitalists can change their factors from one concrete form that is yielding a lower rent to another that promises more. But then it was not supplies of concrete factors that were given, but a quantity of "capital" in the abstract. What is meant by saying that a quantity of "capital" remains the same when it changes its form is a mystery that has never been explained to this day.

Marshall impaled himself upon the other horn of the dilemma. Profit as the supply-price of *waiting* lends itself naturally to the interpretation that a certain rate of profit will induce a certain rate of accumulation. For any rate of growth of an economy there is a particular level of profit normally expected on investment, and in competitive conditions any particular line that promises more than the normal rate will quickly attract more than its share of investment, so as to bring down the return. Contrariwise where prospective profits are below the normal level. Thus a continuous ebb and flow is tending to establish an even level throughout the system. But what Marshall needs is the ratio of profit appropriate to a stock of capital, not to a rate of accumulation. Land, labour and *waiting* are the factors of production; rent, wages and interest their rewards. Yet to treat owning a stock of capital already in being as a "sacrifice," to be added to the "efforts" of the workers, is not really very telling. Marshall left it all rather hazy, and hazy it has been ever since.

It was Professor Pigou who reconciled the two sides of the neo-classical doctrine by placing it in a setting of stationary equilibrium, when accumulation has come to an end. To own any quantity of wealth, measured in purchasing power, the capitalists, in their capacity as rentiers, require a particular rate of interest, corresponding to their marginal rate of discount of future consumption. Given the quantity of wealth in existence, a lower rate of interest would cause them to consume more, a higher rate to save. Also there is a rate of profit at which capitalists in their capacity as entrepreneurs are willing to make use of a stock of concrete capital goods embodying a particular quantity of wealth, the rate of profit being governed by the marginal productivity of capital. Equilibrium exists when the stock of capital is such that the rate of interest that represents its supply-price is equal to the rate of profit that represents its demand-price. In this setting the Walrasian equations can be fitted into place and a unique pattern of prices and quantities appears, the pressure of each part upon the rest holding the whole in balance.

Logical structures of this kind have a certain charm. They allow those without mathematics to catch a hint of what intellectual beauty means. This has been a great support to them in their ideological function. In the face of such elegance, only a philistine could complain that the contemplation of an ultimate stationary state, when accumulation has come to an end, is not going to help us very much with the problems of today.

3

On one point the *laisser-faire* school had a definite political platform. They were strong advocates of Free Trade. This, indeed, had been all along the central doctrine of political economy. Adam Smith's main argument, carrying on where the Physiocrats left off, was directed against Mercantilism. Ricardo's theory of rent led up to the abolition of the corn laws. For the neo-classicals a belief in Free Trade became the very hallmark of an economist; protectionists belonged to the lesser breeds without the law.

The case for Free Trade was basically the same thing as the general case for the individualistic pursuit of profit, though, starting from Ricardo's theory of comparative costs, it was dressed up in a different form. It exhibited an equilibrium position in which competition leads to the maximum *utility* in the world as a whole being produced from given resources.

But, to appeal to the politicians and the voters, the good of the world as a whole was too thin. The argument that protection could benefit one country only at the expense of the rest would not do; the public might have answered: "If it is going to benefit us, lead us to it." Nor was it sufficient to prove, in a hard-headed classical style, that Free Trade would benefit the United Kingdom. It had to be shown that, under it, each and every country would be better off, so that it could be preached round the world with a good conscience. Protectionists are represented as being mere lobbyists for particular interests. A tariff might benefit one trade, but it was bound to do more harm to the rest of the economy than good to those protected. (Scruples about adding *utilities*, making interpersonal comparisons and admitting value judgments were laid aside at this point. Their function was to combat dangerous thoughts on the home front, not to undermine the logical basis of the Free Trade dogma.)

It is true enough that the demand for a tariff more often comes from a lobby than anywhere else, but it is not true that no good national arguments can ever be found for protection.

Let us see how the neo-classical doctrine side-stepped them. A model was set up for the pure theory of international trade, each country being in a static condition, with given population, natural resources, capital stock and technical knowledge. International equilibrium also prevailed, with the value of imports equal to exports. Conditions of full employment and perfect competition are taken for granted. The benefits of trade, as opposed to isolation, are exhibited in terms of this model.

Now, in real life, one reason why nations may resort to protection is to increase employment at home. There is no room for this argument in the pure theory, for full employment obtains already. (Pigou, indeed, allowed that in certain cases the imposition of a tariff may relieve unemployment caused by a failure of the equilibrium position to be established, but he sheltered himself from drawing any positive conclusion from the analysis by quoting Sidgwick's view that, although theory would point out cases where protection might do good, the clumsy hands of government were not to be trusted with the delicate task of picking the right cases.[1])

Again, a country may curtail imports to correct the balance of payments. But in the pure theory there is a mechanism, working through gold flows, that will adjust prices so that imports and exports balance.

Then there is the question of building up home industries so that they can catch up upon foreign producers who for the moment are underselling them. Here it was impossible altogether to prevent common sense breaking in. An exception had to be made for "infant industries." However, they were in one of those empty boxes labelled "increasing returns"; any

[1] *Public Finance*, p. 209.

actual claimant for the status of infant was highly suspect; the idea, nowadays a commonplace, that protection may foster development of industry as a whole in backward countries, was never brought up.

Even so, after all the interesting problems had been ruled out, the case for Free Trade as a benefit to each nation could not be made out. The weak spot in the analysis was in overlooking the implications of the assumption of universal perfect competition. It is obvious enough that any one group of sellers can normally do better for themselves collectively by agreeing to keep up prices than by competing individualistically. They do less business, but at a higher profit per unit. Similarly any one nation, within the conditions of the equilibrium model, may be better off with a smaller volume of trade at higher prices of exports in terms of imports than at the free-trade position. This was pointed out in a now famous article by Bickerdike, criticizing Edgworth in terms of his own diagrammatic analysis. Edgworth was obliged to admit the point, and he advanced the correction to the pure free-trade case that a small tariff may be beneficial.[1] It is a "small" tariff in the same sense as a monopolist makes a "small" increase over the competitive price. The most paying price is not the highest possible price, at which sales would be very much reduced, but that which yields the highest multiple of profit per unit with units sold.

This was a very serious breach in the Free-Trade case. How was it dealt with? It was simply lost to view. Bickerdike's article is now well known, for it was dug out of oblivion when Abba Lerner rediscovered the same point in the Thirties[2] and it has been bandied about a great deal since that time. But till then it was effectively hushed up. In a now-forgotten volume,

---

[1] *Papers Relating to Political Economy*, Vol. II, "Bickerdike's Theory of Incipient Taxes."

[2] "The Diagrammatic Representation of Demand Conditions in International Trade," *Economica*, August 1934.

which represents a low ebb in neo-classical thought, the question is treated as follows —

There is one highly theoretical argument, as to the possible advantage to a country of shifting the terms of trade in its favour (i.e. lowering the prices of what it imports in relation to what it exports) by imposing a tariff, to which no further reference is made in this volume. Those who are interested in these matters may find the argument briefly stated and answered by Professor Jacob Viner in an article on "The Tariff Question and the Economist" in the *Nation and Athenaeum* of 7th February 1931. "No economist, as far as I know" (Professor Viner concludes) "has ever maintained that the gain to any country from the favourable shift in the terms of trade due to Protection is ever likely, under conceivable circumstances, to equal her loss from the uneconomic re-allocation of her productive resources."[1]

The point was, of course, that in the pre-1914 world Great Britain had everything to gain from other nations' adopting free trade and very little to lose from maintaining it herself. The hang-over from pre-war confidence in the doctrine only gave way when unemployment and the chronic weakness of the British balance of trade were so much exaggerated by the world slump as to force even economists to notice that something had changed.

Marshall, the old fox, had known perfectly well that it was all a question of national self-interest —

While recognizing the leadership of Adam Smith, the German economists have been irritated more than any others by what they have regarded as the insular narrowness and self-confidence of the Ricardian school. In particular they resented the way in which the English advocates of free trade tacitly assumed that a proposition which had been established with regard to a manufacturing country, such as England was, could be carried over without modification to agricultural countries. The brilliant genius and national enthusiasm

[1] *Tariffs: The Case Examined*, Sir William Beveridge and Others, p. 14, footnote 1.

of List overthrew this presumption; and showed that the Ricardians had taken but little account of the indirect effects of free trade. No great harm might be done in neglecting them so far as England was concerned; because they were in the main beneficial and thus added to the strength of its direct effects. But he showed that in Germany, and still more in America, many of its indirect effects were evil; and he contended that these evils outweighed its direct benefits.[1]

But this is in a rather boring appendix to the *Principles* on the history of thought, and few of Marshall's pupils were aware that he had ever been so indiscreet as to mention that Free Trade was good for us, but might not be so good for the others.

### 4

With *utility* came mathematics and seemed to promise a new dawn for economics as a truly scientific subject. Ricardo's habit of mind was mathematical but he knew no algebra. For Jevons, mathematics was the key —

> It seems perfectly clear that Economy, if it is to be a science at all, must be a mathematical science. There exists much prejudice against attempts to introduce the methods and language of mathematics into any branch of the moral sciences. Most persons appear to hold that the physical sciences form the proper sphere of mathematical method, and that the moral sciences demand some other method, I know not what. My theory of Economy, however, is purely mathematical in character.
>
> I know not when we shall have a perfect system of statistics, but the want of it is the only insuperable obstacle in the way of making Political Economy an exact Science.[2]

It was Edgworth who made the largest claims. Happiness is to be measured as a two-dimensional quantity, the dimensions being intensity and time, and the unit the minimum sensible increment in either direction. The Utilitarian principle that

---

[1] *Principles*, p. 767.
[2] *Theory of Political Economy* (1st Ed.), p. 3.

policy should be directed to the greatest good for the greatest number requires the summation of the happiness of separate individuals, and Edgworth saw no difficulty —

In virtue of what *unit* is such comparison possible? It is here submitted: Any individual experiencing a unit of pleasure-intensity during a unit of time is to "count for one." Utility, then, has *three* dimensions; a mass of utility, "lot of pleasure" is greater than another when it has more *intensity–time–number* units. The third dimension is doubtless an evolutional acquisition, and is still far from perfectly evolved.

Looking back at our triple scale, we find no peculiar difficulty about the third dimension. It is an affair of census. The second dimension is an affair of clockwork: assuming that the distinction here touched, between subjective and objective measure of time, is of minor importance. But the first dimension, where we leave the safe ground of the objective, equating to unity each *minimum sensible*, presents indeed peculiar difficulties. *Atoms of pleasure* are not easy to distinguish and discern; more continuous than sand, more discrete than liquid; as it were nuclei of the just-perceivable, embedded in circumambient semi-consciousness.

We cannot *count* the golden sands of life; we cannot *number* the "innumerable smile" of seas of love; but we seem to be capable of observing that there is here a *greater*, there a *less*, multitude of pleasure-units, mass of happiness; and that is enough.[1]

This seems to be heading straight for egalitarianism of the most uncompromising kind but Edgworth succeeds in side-stepping —

Of the Utilitarian Calculus the central conception is *Greatest Happiness*, the greatest possible sum-total of pleasure summed through all time and over all sentience. Mathematical reasonings are employed partly to confirm Mr. Sidgwick's proof that Greatest Happiness is the *end* of right action; and partly to deduce middle axioms, *means* conducive to that end. This deduction is of a very abstract, perhaps only negative, character; negativing the assumption that *Equality* is necessarily implied in Utilitarianism. For, if sentients differ in

[1] *Mathematical Psychics*, p. 8.

*Capacity for Happiness*—under similar circumstances some classes of sentients experiencing on an average more pleasure (e.g. of imagination and sympathy) and less pain (e.g. of fatigue) than others — there is no presumption that equality of circumstances is the most felicific arrangement; especially when account is taken of the interests of posterity.[1]

This escape-clause has often been found useful, but it is precisely this that gives the show away. A unit of measurement implies an agreed convention that is the same for everybody. Locked in the individual's subjective consciousness, it is not a unit at all. The unit of happiness is the same kind of mirage as Ricardo's *absolute value* or Marx's *abstract labour*.

This kind of pseudo-mathematics still flourishes today. Quantitative *utility* long since evaporated, but it is still common to set up models in which quantities of "capital" appear, without any indication of what it is supposed to be a quantity of. Just as the problem of giving an operational meaning to *utility* used to be avoided by putting it into a diagram, so the problem of giving a meaning to the quantity of "capital" is evaded by putting it into algebra. $K$ is capital, $\Delta K$ is investment. Then what is $K$? Why, capital of course. It must mean something, so let us get on with the analysis, and do not bother about these officious prigs who ask us to say what it means.

In spite of this heritage of bad habits, economics has profited enormously from the discipline that the marginalists introduced.

Once more metaphysical concepts, that are strictly speaking nonsense, have made a contribution to science. The method of economic analysis is a habit of thought which, to any one who has it, appears mere common sense. He only appreciates it when he starts to argue with someone who has not got it. Mr. Little describes his experiences in Whitehall as follows —

Before I became an economic adviser I found it rather hard to understand why economists were likely to be useful (except in rather

---

[1] Ibid., p. vii.

limited ways). It seemed to me that the basic essential framework of applicable ideas was so simple and limited that any able man concerned with economic affairs could and would acquire them as he went along, without any need of formal training. As soon as one strayed beyond this very limited corpus of thought, economic theory became inapplicable. And as for any really professional methods of prediction — well any sensible economist regards them as exploratory exercises in method rather than as something to be trusted in practice. ...

My experience in Whitehall cured the malaise which derives from thinking one's subject overblown. This is not to say that a knowledge of academic economics is a *sine qua non* for offering good advice on economic affairs. There are first-class practitioners of the art who would not shine in a university seminar. But I was convinced that an extensive knowledge of economic theory and controversy (as well as a quantitative acquaintance with economic facts and some knowledge of modern economic history) is helpful—more helpful than Latin, Logic and Ancient History. ...

Economic theory teaches one how economic magnitudes are related, and how very complex and involved these relationships are. Non-economists tend to be too academic. They abstract too much from the real world. No one can think about economic issues without some theory, for the facts and relationships are too involved to organize themselves: they do not simply fall into place. But if the theorist is untutored, he is apt to construct a very partial theory which blinds him to some of the possibilities. Or he falls back on some old and over-simple theory, picked up from somewhere or other. He is also, I believe, apt to interpret the past naïvely. *Post hoc ergo propter hoc* is seldom an adequate economic explanation. I was sometimes shocked by the naïve sureness with which very questionable bits of economic analysis were advanced in Whitehall.[1]

In its own day, however, the neo-classical scheme was rather barren of results. Jevons started off briskly enough with statistical investigations, but his lead was little followed by other theorists (though much work was done in realistic studies without benefit of theory). Statistical generalizations like

[1] "The Economist in Whitehall", *Lloyds Bank Review*, April 1957, p. 35.

Pareto's so-called law of distribution or the supposed regularity of the trade cycle did not arise out of the central core of analysis and special theories had to be fixed up to explain them.

At the very end of the neo-classical reign Professor Clapham was teasing the economists —

Picture an economist, well-educated in the dominant British school, going over a hat-factory. On the shelves of the store, the first room he enters, are boxes containing hats. On the shelves of his mind are also boxes. There is a row labelled Diminishing Return Industries, Constant Return Industries, Increasing Return Industries. Above that a dustier row labelled Monopolies (with discrimination of three degrees) in Diminishing Return Industries, Constant Return Industries, Increasing Return Industries. On top again he can just read the dockets, Taxes on Monopolies in Diminishing Return Industries — and so on. He is aware that these boxes are not very prominent on the shelves of some economists of whose mental furniture he generally approves; but he received them from his masters and he has seen them handled with beautiful ingenuity by his friends. Yet from all his reading and conversations he cannot recall a scene in which anyone opened the boxes and said, with authority and convincing evidence, "Constant Return Industry, hosen; Increasing Return Industry, hats," or used any like words. Nor can he think of an industrial monograph in which profitable use was made of the Law of Returns in commenting on the things of life. Perhaps he has himself tried to write a little monograph and remembers how, doubtless for lack of wit, he made of them no use; but how for this no one ever blamed him.

He takes down, in memory and when he gets home, from his shelves, *Industry and Trade: A Study of Industrial Technique and Business Organization*, with its nearly nine hundred pages packed full of the things of life. Two references to Constant Returns — one in a footnote — and a handful of references to Diminishing and Increasing Returns *im Allgemeinen*, not so far as he can find in close relation to the facts of those British, French, German and American Industries of which the great book has taught him so much: these seem to be all. He tries *The Economics of Welfare* to find that, in nearly a thousand pages, there is not even one illustration of what industries are in which boxes, though many an argument begins "when conditions of diminishing returns prevail" or "when conditions of increasing returns prevail," as if everyone knew when that was.[1]

There was a twofold reason I think for this sterility.

First, the questions being discussed were of no practical importance. The policy recommended was *laisser faire*, and there was no need to describe in any detail how to do nothing. Maxims for taxation, it is true, emerge from Marshall's analysis but they are an expository device rather than a prescription for policy. Commodities in inelastic demand were in any case being taxed because they yield revenue, and Marshall's argument about consumer's surplus did not add anything. As for Pigou's taxes and subsidies, if anyone had taken them seriously he would have been eagerly searching out increasing and diminishing return industries, and this is just what (as Clapham pointed out) no one was doing.

Apart from the advocacy of Free Trade there was not much to say on practical questions arising out of the central core of the *laisser-faire* theory (as opposed to various miscellaneous questions that were brought up from time to time by passing events); it was because its only concern with politics was negative that theory made so little progress in developing operational concepts that could be used on actual data.

The second reason why the neo-classicals were so much isolated from practice was the dominance of the concept of equilibrium in the theory itself. The function of economic theory, as opposed to economic theology, is to set up hypotheses that can be tested. But if an hypothesis is framed in terms of the position of equilibrium that would be attained when all parties concerned had correct foresight, there is no point in testing it; we know in advance that it will not prove correct. The dominance of equilibrium was excused by the fact that it is excessively complicated to bring into a single model both

[1] "Of Empty Economic Boxes," *Economic Journal*, September 1922.

movements of the whole through time and the detailed inter-
action of the parts. It was necessary for purely intellectual
reasons to choose between a simple dynamic model and an
elaborate static one. But it was no accident that the static one
was chosen; the soothing harmonies of equilibrium supported
*laisser-faire* ideology and the elaboration of the argument kept us
all too busy to have any time for dangerous thoughts.

# IV

## THE KEYNESIAN REVOLUTION

SOME of Keynes' contemporaries and seniors dislike the expression "the Keynesian Revolution." There was nothing, they say, so very new in the *General Theory*.[1] Of course everything can be found in Marshall, even the *General Theory*. But we know what Marshall's pupils who had gone into the Treasury believed, from the famous White Paper of 1929[2] which was an example of neo-classical theory in action. In the General Election of that year Lloyd George was fighting his campaign on a promise to abolish unemployment which had long been above 10 per cent (it rose later to 20 per cent) by a programme of public works. The Treasury (very improperly from a constitutional point of view) was asked to show why this was impossible. Their argument is very simple. The total fund of saving is given, and if more is used for home investment, foreign lending, and consequently the export surplus, would be reduced correspondingly; there would be no advantage to the economy as a whole.[3]

Nowadays this seems merely laughable. It is not necessary now to repeat the familiar tale of the hard-fought victory of the theory of effective demand; we are concerned rather to see the relevance of the new line to the themes that we have been discussing.

[1] They are in a very weak position to say that to the present writer, who learned the pre-Keynesian orthodoxy at their feet.
[2] *Memorandum on Certain Proposals Relating to Unemployment*, Cmd. 3331.
[3] Op. cit., p. 47.

First of all, Keynes brought back something of the hard-headedness of the Classics. He saw the capitalist system as a system, a going concern, a phase in historical development. Sometimes it filled him with rage and despair but on the whole he approved of it or at any rate he felt it worthwhile trying to patch it up and make it work tolerably well. But like Adam Smith's, his defence was based on expediency —

For my part, I think that Capitalism wisely managed, can probably be made more efficient for attaining economic ends than any alternative system yet in sight, but that in itself it is in many ways extremely objectionable. Our problem is to work out a social organization which shall be as efficient as possible without offending our notions of a satisfactory way of life.[1]

Secondly, Keynes brought back the moral problem that *laisser-faire* theory had abolished. It is true that in Cambridge we had never been taught that economics should be *wertfrei* or that the positive and the normative can be sharply divided. We knew that the search was for fruit as well as light. But the anodyne of *laisser faire* had worked pretty thoroughly even in Cambridge. Marshall, certainly, was a great moralizer, but somehow the moral always came out that whatever is, is *very nearly* best. Pigou set out the argument of his *Economics of Welfare* in terms of exceptions to the rule that *laisser faire* ensures maximum satisfaction; he did not question the rule. Readjustments were needed here and there to make the distribution of resources between uses the most efficient possible. The inequality of the distribution of the product raised doubts, but they were easily deflected into Utopian daydreams. Even Keynes, as we have just seen, while he did not much like the profit motive, thought (in the Twenties) that it provided a better mechanism than any other "yet in sight" for operating

---

[1] *Essays in Persuasion*, p. 321.

the economic system, with the reservation that it did not necessarily make the best possible use of its resources.

In the Thirties a large part of its resources were not being used
for anything at all; Keynes diagnosed the cause as a deep-seated
defect in the mechanism, and thereby added an exception to the
comfortable rule that every man in bettering himself was doing
good to the commonwealth, so large as completely to disrupt
the reconciliation of the pursuit of private profit with public
beneficence.

The whole elaborate structure of the metaphysical justification for profit was blown up when he pointed out that capital
yields a return not because it is *productive* but because it is
*scarce*.[1] Still worse, the notion that saving is a cause of unemployment cut the root of the justification for unequal income as a
source of accumulation.

What made the *General Theory* so hard to accept was not its
intellectual content, which in a calm mood can easily be
mastered, but its shocking implications. Worse than private
vices being public benefits, it seemed that the new doctrine
was the still more disconcerting proposition that private
virtues (of thriftiness and careful husbandry) were public
vices.

We have seen our way through this now. When full employment is going to be maintained in any case, saving is
certainly more desirable than spending from a public point of
view. Saving is only bad when investment fails to make use of
it. But at the time Keynes seemed to be upholding a "licentious
system" that was even more objectionable than Mandeville's
had been to Adam Smith. And, of course, Keynes, like Mandeville, was a dreadful tease. He preferred not to coat his tart pills
with any soothing sugar. The nastier, the more good they
would do.

---

[1] *General Theory*, p. 213.

By making it impossible to believe any longer in an automatic reconciliation of conflicting interests into a harmonious whole, the *General Theory* brought out into the open the problem of choice and judgment that the neo-classicals had managed to smother. The ideology to end ideologies broke down. Economics once more became Political Economy.

Thirdly, Keynes brought back *time* into economic theory. He woke the Sleeping Princess from the long oblivion to which "equilibrium" and "perfect foresight" had condemned her and led her out into the world here and now.

This release took economics a great stride forward, away from theology towards science; now it is no longer necessary for hypotheses to be framed in such a form that we know in advance that they will be disproved. Hypotheses relating to a world where human beings actually live, where they cannot know the future or undo the past, have at least in principle the possibility of being set out in a testable form.

2

Keynes was very sceptical of econometrics (it is by no means certain that the work done in the last twenty years would have laid his doubts); but it was he who made the new statistical work possible. In *How to Pay for the War* he used the first National Income tables set out in the modern manner by double entry, in a knock-up which Erwin Rothbarth made for him, and under his influence the method was officially accepted and is now universally established.

The descent into time has brought economic theory also into touch with history. Keynes himself lacked the scruple of a scholar. He would pick up any example to illustrate a thesis, and if one betrayed him he could always find another. He made wild suggestions, such as that Shakespeare's genius could have flourished only in an age of inflation,[1] or that civilization cannot be found except where there were earthquakes to lead from time to time to a reconstruction boom.[2] These light-hearted arguments were only superficial ornaments to point the paradoxes of analysis. (He planned to take up economic history seriously at the age of seventy, and we cannot know how he would have turned out at it.) Though Keynes himself was no historian, the *General Theory* has opened up a great field for an analytical survey of economic history. Formerly there was almost no link between history and theory except the now discredited interpretation of price movements in terms of the supply of gold.

In history, we learned that the mainspring of development was technical inventions; in theory, most of the exercises were in terms of a "given state of knowledge." Inventions were a special, difficult question; even when it was tackled, the argument was conducted by comparing two positions, with different states of knowledge, each already in equilibrium. (Schumpeter, who brought a bowdlerized edition of Marx into academic doctrine, made his system hinge on inventions, but he was some way from the centre of orthodoxy; it was only after Keynes had broken the bounds that he could find a place in it.) In history, we learned of the growth and decay of economic systems; in theory, there was one set of principles that governed life on Robinson Crusoe's island, and among the mythical peasants who bartered cloth for wine, as much as in the City of London or in Chicago.

In history, nations are of various shapes and sizes, with various geographical features and social traditions; in theory there were only A and B, each with an endowment of factors identical in all respects except their relative quantities, trading in identical goods.

[1] *Treatise on Money*, Vol. II, p. 154.
[2] *General Theory*, p. 129.

In history, every event has its consequences, and the question What would have happened if that event had not occurred? is only an idle speculation; in theory there is one position of equilibrium that a system will arrive at, no matter where it starts.

The *General Theory* broke through the unnatural barrier and brought history and theory together again. But for theorists the descent into time has not been easy. After twenty years, the awakened Princess is still dazed and groggy.

Keynes himself was not quite steady on his feet. His remark about the timeless multiplier[1] is highly suspicious. And the hard core of analysis, round which his flashing controversy wheels, is based upon comparisons of static short-period equilibrium positions each with a given rate of investment going on, though it purports to trace the effect of a change in the rate of investment taking place at a moment of time.

Keynes was interested only in very short-period questions (he used to say: "The long period is a subject for under-graduates") and so for him the distinction between making comparisons of the structure of different positions and tracing the consequences of change was perhaps not so very important, though there was a tremendous amount of bally-ragging be-tween him and Sir Dennis Robertson over the point.[2] But when it comes to long-run questions the distinction is indispen-sable, and those who learned to float in the smooth waters of equilibrium find the requirements of historical analysis very uncomfortable. We are still slipping and floundering about like ducks who have alighted on a pond and found it frozen over.

We have broken out of static equilibrium at least in con-nexion with the accumulation of capital. We have learned to distinguish the desire to save from the inducement to invest and

---

[1] *General Theory*, p. 122.
[2] *See* H. G. Johnson, "Some Cambridge Controversies on Monetary Theory," *Review of Economic Studies*, 1951–2, XIX (2) 49.

both from the supply price of a stock of waiting. In other branches of economics the replacement of timeless equilibrium by historical development has still a long struggle before it.

Keynes himself was not interested in the theory of relative prices. Gerald Shove used to say that Maynard had never spent the twenty minutes necessary to understand the theory of value. On these topics he was content to leave orthodoxy alone. He carried a good deal of Marshallian luggage with him and never thoroughly unpacked it to throw out the clothes he could not wear. The Keynesian revolution is only now slowly fighting its way into this terrain.

3

Progress is slow partly from mere intellectual inertia. In a subject where there is no agreed procedure for knocking out errors, doctrines have a long life. A professor teaches what he was taught, and his pupils, with a proper respect and reverence for teachers, set up a resistance against his critics for no other reason than that it was he whose pupils they were.

We have a well-documented example in the case of Pigou and Marshall. Pigou's review of the *General Theory*[1] was harsh and intemperate in tone and, as he afterwards admitted, incorrect in logic. The reason for this performance was that he was deeply grieved and outraged by the way Keynes attacked Marshall.

If he had wanted to be, it would have been easy for Keynes to be "generous" to Marshall, in the way Marshall was to Ricardo, that is to say, to saddle him with his own ideas; Marshall's ambiguities lend themselves even better than Ricardo's to various interpretations. But Keynes, who (unlike Adam Smith's poets) was singularly free of spitefulness because his own self-assurance needed no external nourishment, went

---

[1] *Economica*, May 1936.

out of his way to pick out the interpretation of Marshall most adverse to his own views, to pulverize it, mock it and dance upon the mangled remains, just because he thought it a matter of great importance — of real, urgent, political importance — that people should know that he was saying something fresh. If he had been polite and smooth, if he had used proper scholarly caution and academic reserve, his book would have slipped down unnoticed and millions of families rotting in unemployment would be so much the further from relief. He wanted the book to stick in the gizzards of the orthodox, so that they would be forced either to spew it out or chew it properly.

Pigou spewed it out, not, I am sure, because disobliging remarks in it are made about himself, but because his loyalty to Marshall was outraged.

When he happened to pick the book up thirteen years later, and read it calmly, he was amazed to find that he agreed with most of it, and that his review had done Keynes wrong. He had retired, and Keynes was dead, but he asked to be allowed to give two lectures to the undergraduates, to make reparation to Keynes for his unfair review.[1] For the young men, to whom I suppose the *General Theory* is just another of those classics that you hope your tutor will not notice that you have not read, it was rather mystifying; for those who had lived through the old battles, it was a moving and noble scene.

It provides us now with an exceptionally clear-cut example of how personal sentiment can build up a defence for old ideas against new.

There is, of course, a purely intellectual element as well. New ideas are difficult just because they are new. Repetition has somehow plastered over the gaps and inconsistencies in the old ones, and the new cannot penetrate. It needs a bulldozer as forceful as Keynes to break a way in.

There is also a psychological element in the survival of

[1] *See* "Keynes' *General Theory*, A Retrospective View."

equilibrium theory. There is an irresistible attraction about the concept of equilibrium — the almost silent hum of a perfectly running machine; the apparent stillness of the exact balance of counteracting pressures; the automatic smooth recovery from a chance disturbance. Is there perhaps something Freudian about it? Does it connect with a longing to return to the womb? We have to look for a psychological explanation to account for the powerful influence of an idea that is intellectually unsatisfactory.

4

The concept of equilibrium, of course, is an indispensable tool of analysis. Even Marx makes use of the case of "simple reproduction" to clear the ground for his analysis of accumulation in terms of saving and investment; simple reproduction, where the stock of all capital goods is being kept intact, has a great deal in common with Pigou's "thorough-going stationary state." But to use the equilibrium concept one has to keep it in its place, and its place is strictly in the preliminary stages of an analytical argument, not in the framing of hypotheses to be tested against the facts, for we know perfectly well that we shall not find facts in a state of equilibrium. Yet many writers seem to conceive the long-period as a date somewhere in the future that we shall get to some day. Or even suggest that if it can be shown that in equilibrium something is true — say imports equal exports, or profits are at a normal rate — then it somehow does not much matter that every day, now and to come, it will not be true. To take a contemporary example of this way of arguing — it is said that in the long run every monopoly will break down.[1] This seems to be a rash generalization, but that is not the point. The point is that this argument is used to suggest

[1] Peter Wiles, "Are Adjusted Roubles Rational?" *Soviet Studies*, Oct. 1955 p. 144.

that the phenomenon of monopoly profit is not important, in spite of the fact that on every particular day that the sun shines, a number of monopolies that have not yet broken down will be merrily making hay. "In the long run we are all dead," but not all of us at once.

Long-run equilibrium is a slippery eel. Marshall evidently intended to mean by the long period a horizon which is always at a certain distance in the future, and this is a useful metaphor; but he slips into discussing a position of equilibrium which is shifted by the very process of approaching it and he got himself into a thorough tangle by drawing three-dimensional positions on a plane diagram.[1]

No one would deny that to speak of a tendency towards equilibrium that itself shifts the position towards which it is tending is a contradiction in terms. And yet it still persists. It is for this reason that we must attribute its survival to some kind of psychological appeal that transcends reason.

Marshall was very well aware of the difficulty of making generalizations intended to apply to actual life in terms of timeless concepts. Normal price is the "value which economic forces would bring about if the general conditions of life were stationary for a run of time long enough to enable them all to work out their full effect."[2]

Sir Dennis Robertson, thinking it mere perversity in a critic not to be satisfied with this, indignantly repeats it.[3] But how if the economic forces present in a particular situation are mutually contradictory? Say, part of the investment that is being carried out is the result of expectations of profit which another part is going to make unobtainable? What is the equilibrium that the working out of these forces would lead to if it had time enough to get there? And in any case do "stationary conditions" apply

[1] *Principles*, Appendix H.
[2] *Principles*, p. 347.
[3] *Lectures on Economic Principles*, Vol. I, p. 95.

to a given population and stock of capital, or a given rate of growth or a given acceleration of growth?

Even if these conundrums could be answered and a definite meaning given to the passage through time of the normal point towards which the actual position is tending to move, we ought to inquire how far off from equilibrium the actual position tends to be — how fast is the reaction towards normal, compared to the speed of movement of the normal position? In what cases is the gap growing, in what narrowing? These are interesting and important questions, but except in the special department — trade-cycle theory — where the Keynesian revolution commands the field, they are seldom posed, let alone answered. The argument stops when normal position has been described and the equilibrium lullaby hushes further inquiry.

5

These are subsidiary reasons for the survival and revival of pre-Keynesian ideas. The main reason, as always, we must look for in the ideological sphere. Keynes brought back the moral problem into economics by destroying the neo-classical reconciliation of private egoism and public service. He also exposed another weakness. There is another conflict in human life, akin to the conflict between the interests of myself and the others — that is the conflict between myself now and in the future. This conflict the neo-classical ideology did not really resolve; rather it was evaded. Prudence is something akin to virtue and needs the exercise of self-command. The concept of *waiting* as a sacrifice is connected with the view that any owner of wealth is under a constant temptation to consume it in "present gratifications" and interest is the "reward" that leads him to refrain.

Because the neo-classical system was always so hazy about an economy as a whole and kept the spotlight on relative prices, it was able to leave the crucial question of the proper rate of saving in this unsatisfactory state. If I discount the future, then, when that future day becomes the present, I shall kick myself. Is the optimum rate of saving for society to be trusted to such chuckle-headed types? And what about posterity? Family feeling is a weak prop, for it is precisely the bachelors who have the biggest margin for saving. It was partly as a refuge from these awkward questions that the stationary state in which accumulation has come to an end was so valuable to Marshall's successors.

Ten years before the *General Theory*, Keynes had pronounced the funeral oration on *laisser faire* —

Let us clear from the ground the metaphysical or general principles upon which, from time to time, *laissez-faire* has been founded. It is *not* true that individuals possess a prescriptive "natural liberty" in their economic activities. There is *no* "compact" conferring perpetual rights on those who Have or on those who Acquire. The world is *not* so governed from above that private and social interest always coincide. It is *not* so managed here below that in practice they coincide. It is *not* a correct deduction from the Principles of Economics that enlightened self-interest always operates in the public interest. Nor is it true that self-interest generally *is* enlightened; more often individuals acting separately to promote their own ends are too ignorant or too weak to attain even these. Experience does *not* show that individuals, when they make up a social unit, are always less clear-sighted than when they act separately.

We cannot, therefore, settle on abstract grounds, but must handle on its merits in detail, what Burke termed "one of the finest problems in legislation, namely, to determine what the State ought to take upon itself to direct by the public wisdom, and what it ought to leave, with as little interference as possible, to individual exertion." We have to discriminate between what Bentham, in his forgotten but useful nomenclature, used to term *Agenda* and *Non-Agenda*, and to do this without Bentham's prior presumption that interference is, at the same time, "generally needless" and "generally pernicious."[1]

[1] *Essays in Persuasion*, pp. 312–13.

In *The End of Laissez-faire* Keynes had only this to say on the question of accumulation —

My second example relates to Savings and Investment. I believe that some co-ordinated act of intelligent judgment is required as to the scale on which it is desirable that the community as a whole should save, the scale on which these savings should go abroad in the form of foreign investments, and whether the present organization of the investment market distributes savings along the most nationally productive channels. I do not think that these matters should be left entirely to the chances of private judgment and private profits, as they are at present.[1]

When the whole question of seeing that potential savings are not run to waste in unemployment, that the investible resources shall be used, is added to the *agenda*, it seems as if there is precious little *non-agenda* left.

To dispute the main point has become impossible. But Keynes himself had moments of nostalgia for the old doctrines.

"The Social Philosophy towards which the General Theory might lead" is markedly less radical than the argument of the book has led the reader to expect —

Our criticism of the accepted classical theory of economics has consisted not so much in finding logical flaws in its analysis as in pointing out that its tacit assumptions are seldom or never satisfied, with the result that it cannot solve the economic problems of the actual world. But if our central controls succeed in establishing an aggregate volume of output corresponding to full employment as nearly as is practicable, the classical theory comes into its own again from this point onwards. If we suppose the volume of output to be given, i.e. to be determined by forces outside the classical scheme of thought, then there is no objection to be raised against the classical analysis of the matter in which private self-interest will determine what in particular is produced, in what proportions the factors of production will be combined to produce it, and how the value of the final product will be distributed between them.[2]

[1] Ibid., p. 318.
[2] *General Theory*, p. 378.

In this diminished kingdom *laisser faire* can still flourish; from this ground it can make sallies to recapture lost territory. It is this rallying of the old ideological forces round their oriflamme — the optimum distribution of resources in long-period equilibrium — that accounts for the slow progress that has been made in bringing the so-called theory of Value and Distribution into touch with historic time and the so-called theory of Welfare into touch with human life.

6

In some ways the unkindest cut of all was Keynes' repudiation of the doctrine that tariffs must be harmful to the country that imposes them. He did not delve into the pure theory and the Bickerdike argument. He was interested in the much simpler and more straightforward point that a tariff which deflects demand from foreign to home goods increases employment in home industries.

Keynes, brought up in the strictest sect of the Pharisees, had been a dogmatic Free-Trader in his day. With his usual lack of patriotism for his own past ideas he chooses himself in the *General Theory* as the exponent of the doctrine that he now wants to attack —

It will be fairest, perhaps, to quote, as an example, what I wrote myself. So lately as 1923, as a faithful pupil of the classical school who did not at that time doubt what he had been taught and entertained on this matter no reserves at all, I wrote: "If there is one thing that protection can *not* do, it is to cure Unemployment ... There are some arguments for Protection, based upon its securing possible but improbable advantages, to which there is no simple answer. But the claim to cure Unemployment involves the Protectionist fallacy in its grossest and crudest form."[1]

[1] Ibid., p. 334.

This was not really part of the formal doctrine, for the Free-Trade case was argued in terms of a model that took full employment for granted, but it was certainly part of the "vulgar economics" which was being taught at that time.

In the work already quoted as marking the low ebb of neo-classical thought it is argued, first, that "We cannot, by cutting off imports, avoid in the long run cutting off a comparable value of exports that we should otherwise have made."[1] (On this argument the foreign investment which was the glory of our nineteenth-century economy just could not have happened.) Second, that we *could* have a surplus of exports, but that this would mean investing abroad instead of in our own country,[2] and finally, that if anything is to be done about unemployment it would be better to do it by investment at home in housing and roads. The last argument, of course, had much to recommend it (though in the circumstances of the time some protection, or devaluation, would have been a necessary adjunct to public-works policy). But as the authors of this polemic see it, it is the Chinese-famine excuse: Why should I subscribe to famine relief in China when so many of our own people are in want? I will not subscribe to anything at all.

Opinions may differ among Free Traders, as amongst others, as to how far it is wise to press such schemes of public expenditure and how far they will merely delay natural and necessary re-adjustments. But the fundamental case for Free Trade remains unshaken by the demonstration that there is a standing pool of unemployed factors of production: for Free Trade ensures that such amount of the factors of production as the wage policy of trade unions and the conditions of investment and enterprise between them allow to be employed, are at least not utilized in producing things which can more easily be obtained by exchange, in accord with the principles of international division of labour.[3]

[1] *Tariffs, the Case Examined*, p. 53.
[2] Loc. cit., p. 56.
[3] Op. cit., p. 74.

This once more illustrates how little logic an ideology really needs. The great outcry against Keynes' treachery to the Free-Trade cause, which made strong men weep, shows how long an ideology can survive its usefulness; the doctrines that, at least from a patriotic point of view, it was desirable to preach when England was the greatest exporting nation, made precious little sense at any level in the nineteen-thirties.

The Free-Trade doctrine is the clearest case of how the moral problem was abolished by the neo-classicals and how the Keynesian revolution brought it back. In the Free-Trade doctrine, with Bickerdike's objection forgotten and Marshall's reservations unread, it seemed that virtue and self-interest were indivisible. Free Trade is not only good for the world as a whole, but for each and every nation. No nation can do itself any good, either by exporting unemployment to the others, restoring its balance of trade or gaining an advantage in prices. National self-interest points to policies which benefit everybody. The advantages claimed for protection are a pure illusion.

Keynes spoilt this happy concatenation of selfish and altruistic motives and plunged us back into an uncomfortable reality, where the more there is of mine the less there is of yours.

7

Within the territory that it has captured, the *General Theory* has made possible a great advance in the direction of science, yet it well illustrates the thesis that ideas are first conceived in a metaphysical form. Liquidity preference bears the same relation to the demand for money in terms of the rate of interest as *utility* does to the demand for commodities in terms of purchasing power, and (like commodities and purchasing power) money and the rate of interest themselves turn out to be unseizable concepts when we really try to pin them down. The constancy of the marginal propensity to consume based on a universal psychological law turns out to have been mere wishful thinking, and a genuinely operational definition of the marginal efficiency of capital is still to seek. Yet without these concepts it is hard to see how the *General Theory* could ever have got on to its feet.

Here the metaphysics is, so to say, a weak infusion, and it does not take much trouble to wring it out. The great ideology-bearing concept in the *General Theory* is Full Employment itself.

Consider first the questions of definition.

When he is concerned with practical policy, Keynes talks of a "satisfactory" level of employment and in the White Paper of 1944,[1] which marked official recognition of the victory of the Keynesian revolution (though even then the Treasury could not quite swallow it), the Government accepts responsibility for the maintenance of a "high and stable" level of employment.

This kind of vagueness is obviously prudent when an aim of policy is being declared. To be too definite is giving hostages to malcontents. Also in the scientific sphere vagueness is more accurate than precision. As Professor Popper points out, science can operate perfectly well with vague terms such as "wind," and when a narrower range of meaning is to be specified, it is done by stating limits — "say 'wind of a velocity of between 20 and 40 miles an hour'." "In physical measurements," he says, "we always take care to consider the range within which there may be an error; and precision does not consist in trying to reduce the range to nothing, or in pretending that there is no such range, but rather in its explicit recognition."[2]

Full employment is bound to be a vague conception. First there is a quite arbitrary element in the hours per week that constitute full time. Does the opportunity to do occasional overtime come in? and if so, how much? Then there is the

---

[1] Cmd. 6527.
[2] *The Open Society and its Enemies*, Vol. II, p. 18.

question of the number of bodies constituting the available labour force at any moment. Married women, students, wealthy rentiers — who is and who is not part of the labour force? Then there is the whole problem of self-employment. The term "disguised unemployment" was originally invented to cover the case of the match-seller in the Strand who appeared during the slump. It has been extended to cover peasants with too small a holding to keep their families productively busy. But how productive? Unemployment shades over into low output per head. None of this matters for positive analysis. The terms can be defined for each problem in the manner appropriate to the matter to be discussed and need be given no more precision than the question requires.

For an ideological slogan this vagueness will not do. Full Employment is a Good Thing, and it is conceived to be attainable by wise policy. It is a blessed state, like equilibrium. We must be able to say what it is.

In his original definition, Keynes distinguishes voluntary unemployment, which may be due to the "withdrawal of their labour by a body of workers because they do not choose to work for less than a certain real reward" and involuntary unemployment —

Men are involuntarily unemployed if, in the event of a small rise in the price of wage-goods relatively to the money-wage, both the aggregate supply of labour willing to work for the current money-wage and the aggregate demand for it at that wage would be greater than the existing volume of employment.[1]

Again —

We have full employment when output has risen to a level at which the marginal return from a representative unit of the factors of production has fallen to the minimum figure at which a quantity of the factors sufficient to produce this output is available.[2]

[1] *General Theory*, p. 15.
[2] Ibid., p. 303

It is the "marginal disutility of labour" that "sets an upper limit"[1] to the potential output.

The disutility of labour is a piece of Marshallian luggage that Keynes thoughtlessly carried with him.

Marshall describes a boy picking blackberries, who goes on until the *marginal utility* of another berry would not be sufficient to repay the *marginal disutility* of the extra effort.[2] In short, he goes on until he feels inclined to stop.

For a worker in a world without social insurance, who has the choice between taking a job at the going wage or having no wage at all, this conception is very much off the mark. Perhaps the reason that Marshall failed to notice its absurdity is connected with the peculiar system of remuneration of Oxford and Cambridge dons. A Fellow gets his college dividend quite independently of the number of units of effort that he puts forth, and he can also take pupils at so much a head. We all know how the marginal disutility of pupils increases with their number, and, with a basic income independently given, differences in the marginal utility of income may be assumed to be less important.

To a college Fellow it is an attractive idea to separate the marginal utility of income from the disutility of work experimentally. Pay him a larger and larger basic salary, and then see how the rate per head required to induce him to take a given number of pupils has to be varied. But unfortunately it would not really be scientific. The value of leisure is not independent of disposable purchasing power. The disutility of work may actually be negative if the alternative is nothing to do and nowhere to go, and is very high when the alternative is delightful, expensive treats.

Any measure that can be proposed for disutility of work will turn out to be elastic. Of all the concepts in the neo-classical bag

---

[1] Ibid., p. 26.
[2] *Principles*, p. 331.

this is the most irremediably metaphysical. Keynes did not attach any importance to it and was quite ready to accept as an alternative a simple-minded definition — that there is full employment when everyone who wants to has a job. But this is an unattainable upper limit. From an ideological standpoint it will not do to say that Full Employment can never be achieved.

Beveridge proposed the criterion of the relation between the number of unfilled vacancies and of registered unemployed. Both figures are obviously very rough indicators of what they are intended to indicate and, even if they were quite exact, an over-all equality between them would not represent a critical point in the relation of supply and demand for labour, since the very coincidence of unfilled vacancies and unemployed workers shows that they do not fit, either because they are geographically separated or because the vacancies are for particular types of work which the unemployed cannot offer. A growing or falling excess of vacancies over unemployed is quite a useful indication, over the short run, of the movements of demand, and a drop in both would presumably indicate an improvement in the general conditions of mobility of labour or versatility of management. But there can be no virtue in taking an exact balance between them to indicate "Full Employment" with capital letters.

(To digress for a moment, it is remarkable that when Beveridge was writing *Full Employment in a Free Society* in consultation with a number of young Keynesians, an *average* of unemployment of three per cent seemed quite a daring objective to propose. The idea that for more than twelve years we should not touch that figure, indeed that two per cent should come to be considered dangerously high, would at that time have seemed extravagant wishful thinking.)

From the first it was obvious that if we ever reached and maintained a low level of unemployment, with the same insti-

tutions of free wage bargaining and the same code of proper
behaviour for trade unions that then obtained, the vicious spiral
of rising prices, wages, prices would become chronic. Already
at that time it could be argued that "the point of full employment, so far from being an equilibrium resting place, appears
to be a precipice over which, once it has reached the edge, the
value of money must plunge into a bottomless abyss."[1] This
has turned out to be sadly true, and it is very troublesome
ideologically, for both Full Employment and stable prices are
Good Things. The solution sometimes found is to say that when
wages are rising there is *overfull* employment and to define Full
Employment so as to include enough unemployment to prevent
money-wage rates from rising faster than productivity. This is
generally accompanied by the arbitrary assumption that some
definite figure, say three per cent of unemployment, would
keep prices stable and by the suggestion that this is a right and
proper policy to aim at maintaining the postulated level.[2]

Michal Kalecki, who discovered the *General Theory* independently, drew from it less optimistic conclusions than Keynes.
When during the war it became clear that the new theory was
firmly established and that the old trade cycle could be overcome, he predicted that we should find ourselves living under
a political trade cycle —

In the slump, either under the pressure of the masses, or even
without it, public investment financed by borrowing will be undertaken to prevent large-scale unemployment. But if attempts are made
to apply this method in order to maintain the high level of employment reached in the subsequent boom a strong opposition of "business
leaders" is likely to be encountered. As has already been argued
lasting full employment is not at all to their liking. The workers
would "get out of hand" and the "captains of industry" would be

[1] Joan Robinson, *Essays in the Theory of Employment*, p. 24.
[2] Cf. J. E. Meade, *The Control of Inflation*. *See also* K. J. C. Knowles and C. B.
Winster, "Can the Level of Unemployment Explain Changes in Wages?"
*Oxford Institute of Statistics Bulletin*, May 1959.

anxious to "teach them a lesson." Moreover, the price increase in the up-swing is to the disadvantage of small and big *rentiers* and makes them "boom tired."

In this situation a powerful block is likely to be formed between big business and the *rentier* interests, and they would probably find more than one economist to declare that the situation was manifestly unsound. The pressure of all these forces, and in particular of big business — as a rule influential in Government departments — would most probably induce the Government to return to the orthodox policy of cutting down the budget deficit. A slump would follow in which Government spending policy would come again into its own. ...

The régime of the "political business cycle" would be an artificial restoration of the position as it existed in nineteenth-century capitalism. Full employment would be reached only at the top of the boom, but slumps would be relatively mild and short lived.[1]

Perhaps more emphasis should have been placed on the City than on big business, and more emphasis on monetary policy than budget deficits, but on the whole the above has proved to have been pretty near the mark.

All the same, the objection to low unemployment has turned out to be relatively weak (at least in Great Britain); certainly any return to heavy unemployment would be violently resisted. Taking it by and large, Full Employment has become an orthodox objective of policy.

The notion that Full Employment is attainable has become, as Keynes in some moods intended it to be, the new defence of *laisser faire*. It is only necessary to remove one glaring defect from the private-enterprise system and it becomes once more an ideal.

Full Employment (with some reservations about not allow-ing it to get *overfull*) has become an aim of Conservative policy

[1] "Political Aspects of Full Employment," *The Political Quarterly*, Oct./Dec. 1943.

and the strongest argument against socialist critics. "You used to complain, we now admit with some justification, that a capitalist system that permits heavy and chronic unemployment is indefensible. Now we offer you capitalism with a high and stable level of employment. You have nothing to complain of."

Marxist critics have understood that Keynes' theory leads to conclusions which from their point of view are reactionary. They therefore deny the logic of his analysis and even find themselves in alliance with the protagonists of the humbug of finance which Keynes first attacked. For instance, Professor Baran is not content with showing that an economic system that can maintain prosperity only by expenditure on armaments is a menace to humanity, morally abhorrent and politically disreputable; he also has to bring in the Quantity Theory of Money to show that it cannot work because Government expenditure causes inflation.[1]

This is another example of confusion between logic and ideology. Because Keynes has shown a way for the capitalist system to remove its most obvious defect, he is a reactionary and therefore his theory is false.

But if his theory were false it would be quite harmless. Just because the diagnosis was correct, the treatment is found to work and the life of the patient is being prolonged, disconcerting his would-be heirs.

The reason why Full Employment has become a right-wing slogan is that if employment is an end in itself no questions can be asked about its content. What is work for? Only to keep the workers out of mischief. Any product is as good as any other.

Keynes fired off his paradoxes to penetrate the thick walls of obscurantism of the old *laisser-faire* orthodoxy —

Ancient Egypt was doubly fortunate, and doubtless owed to this its fabled wealth, in that it possessed *two* activities, namely, pyramid-

---

[1] *The Political Economy of Growth*, p. 124.

building as well as the search for the precious metals, the fruits of which, since they could not serve the needs of man by being consumed, did not stale with abundance. The Middle Ages built cathedrals and sang dirges. Two pyramids, two masses for the dead, are twice as good as one; but not so two railways from London to York. Thus we are so sensible, have schooled ourselves to so close a semblance of prudent financiers, taking careful thought before we add to the "financial" burdens of posterity by building them houses to live in, that we have no such easy escape from the sufferings of unemployment.[1]

And he argues in favour of waste when no useful outlet for investment is seen to be profitable —

In so far as millionaires find their satisfaction in building mighty mansions to contain their bodies when alive and pyramids to shelter them after death, or, repenting of their sins, erect cathedrals and endow monasteries or foreign missions, the day when abundance of capital will interfere with abundance of output may be postponed. "To dig holes in the ground," paid for out of savings, will increase, not only employment, but the real national dividend of useful goods and services.

But he adds —

It is not reasonable, however, that a sensible community should be content to remain dependent on such fortuitous and often wasteful mitigations when once we understand the influences upon which effective demand depends.[2]

Nowadays the paradoxes are taken in sober earnest and building weapons that become obsolete faster than they can be constructed has turned out far better than pyramids ever did to keep up profit without adding to wealth. The relapse on Wall Street that follows any symptom of relaxation in the Cold War is a clear demonstration of the correctness of Keynes' theory,

[1] *General Theory*, p. 131.
[2] Ibid., p. 220.

but also a demonstration of the falsity of his optimistic view that, when the theory was understood, reason would prevail.

He was himself partly to blame for the perversion of his ideas, for he failed to see that, once the principle has been established that maintaining employment is a public concern, the question of what employment shall be for becomes a political issue.

In the last chapter of the *General Theory*, quoted above,[1] he falls into the fallacy of supposing that there is some kind of *neutral* policy that a Government can pursue, to maintain effective demand in general, without having any influence upon any particular demand for anything. The Government has to undertake "the task of adjusting to one another the propensity to consume and the inducement to invest" but everything else is best left to "the free play of economic forces."[2]

This is a metaphysical conception as unseizable as *abstract labour* or *total utility*. What is a policy which *merely* adjusts the demand for investable resources to the supply?

To increase effective demand when it threatens to flag, various means can be used: to reduce taxation or to shift the burden from those most likely to increase their consumption to those most likely to reduce their savings; to foster competition so as to reduce profit margins; to increase subsidies or outlays on social services — all means which tend to reduce inequalities in consumption. Or Government expenditure on investment can be increased, directly or through nationalized industries, or reductions in taxation and credit policy can be used to encourage private investment. Contrariwise, when effective demand seems excessive, taxes to discourage consumption, credit restriction and reduced Government expenditure can be brought into play. And all this has to be worked out so as to preserve the balance of trade at some level or other, as well as to preserve employment. What is a *neutral* policy? What mixture of these

[1] See p. 85.
[2] *General Theory*, pp. 379 and 380.

means is it that leaves private enterprise unaffected in content and acts only on the quantity ?

There is in some quarters a great affection for credit policy because it seems the least selective and somehow lives up to the ideal of a single overall neutral regulation of the economy. The enormous ideological attraction of the Quantity Theory of Money, that kept it going for nearly forty years after its logical content was exploded,[1] is due to the fact that it conceals the problem of political choice under an apparently impersonal mechanism.

Recent experiments have shown, however, that there is no such thing as a purely quantitative, overall financial policy. We are fortunate in having had an official report that finally discards the old mumbo jumbo. But just because the Radcliffe Committee is clear on this point it has no definite recommendations to make. There is no simple right policy; it is all a matter of judgment.

The Keynesian revolution has destroyed the old soporific doctrines, and its own metaphysics is thin and easy to see through. We are left in the uncomfortable situation of having to think for ourselves.

[1] In Keynes' *Tract on Monetary Reform*.

# V

## DEVELOPMENT
## AND UNDER-DEVELOPMENT

AFTER the war, when the problem of deficient effective demand seemed to have faded into the background, a fresh question came to the fore — long-run development.

The change arose partly from the internal evolution of economics as an academic subject. The solution of one problem opens up the next; once Keynes' short-period theory had been established, in which investment plays the key role, it was evidently necessary to discuss the consequences of the accumulation of capital that investment brings about.

Still more, the change in the centre of interest was due to urgent problems thrown up by the actual situation. The nations of the world appeared to be divided into three groups (with some exceptional cases in each). One comprised advanced industrial economies, whose inhabitants enjoy a relatively high level of *per capita* consumption (in terms of goods and services purchased), competing amongst themselves with varying fortunes, with overall average output growing at a moderate rate. Another comprised still largely agricultural economies industrializing at a rapid rate under socialist institutions. And the last, a various group of colonial, neo-colonial and ex-colonial regimes, many experiencing a violent population explosion as a result of importing a modernized death-rate into regions where a primitive birth-rate still obtains, clamouring to escape from the status of hewers of wood and drawers of water for the prosperous West and to set up as prosperous nations themselves.

In this situation both static neo-classical analysis of the

allocation of given resources between various uses, and Keynesian short-period analysis of how given resources are employed,
appear quite inadequate. A dynamic long-run analysis of how
resources can be increased is now what we require.

I

Looking back to traditional teaching for some light on the
question of long-run development, we find on every hand
predictions that the rate of profit will tend to fall and the
accumulation of capital come to an end. A number of quite
different reasons are put forward for this view; none of them
nowadays appears to be cogent.

For Ricardo, the trouble lies in the limitation of natural
resources. In the simplest version of his theory, capital accumu-
lates, offering employment to an ever-growing labour force
(supplied by increasing population) at a fixed wage rate in
terms of corn (which stands for agricultural produce in general).
To increase the output of corn, it is necessary to extend cultivation to inferior lands. The profit per man employed is the excess
over the corn-wage of the net product per man on the land of
lowest yield (the advantage of superior land going entirely to
its owners in the form of rent). Since the net product per man
falls as cultivation is extended, and the corn-value of capital
per man employed is more likely to rise than to fall, the rate of
profit on capital is falling as time goes by. In the end, the motive
for further investment will disappear and accumulation will
come to an end.

Considering the rate at which the population of the world is
growing, all aspiring to attain to the *per capita* level of destruction of natural resources now prevailing in the United States, it
seems as though Ricardo's problem may well become actual
before long. But meanwhile agriculture finds itself suffering
from a failure of effective demand to expand as fast as physical
production, more often than the reverse.

Marx took over the orthodox theory of a falling tendency in the rate of profit and supplied a reason of his own to account for it. According to his explanation, the organic composition of capital tends to rise as time goes by, which may be interpreted to mean that the value of capital per man employed (reckoned in terms of labour-time) is in general increasing because of a capital-using bias in technical progress. The share in the proceeds of industry going to net profit does not rise as fast as the value of capital per man. Consequently the rate of profit on capital is falling. It is possible to attack this proposition on logical grounds[1] but it is simpler to reject its empirical foundation. It is true that physical capital per man, measured in horse-power or tons of steel, is raised by modern technology but, since output per head can rise just as fast in producing capital equipment as in using it, there is no necessary reason why the value of capital per man, in Marx's sense, should increase; in recent times it seems, if anything, to have been falling.

The neo-classical scheme is set out in terms of the equilibrium position of an economy in a "given state of technical knowledge"; an invention is treated as a shock that bounces the economy from one equilibrium to another.

Comparing equilibrium positions it can be shown, from the definition of "given knowledge," that the uses to which capital is put are less profitable the greater the quantity of capital per man (though in what terms the quantity is to be reckoned is usually left very vague). The argument then proceeds from the comparison of equilibrium positions to the suggestion that the accumulation of capital, considered as a process taking place through time, must be accompanied by a falling rate of profit. The transition from a comparison to a process, however, begs all the questions that ought to be discussed.

[1] Cf. Joan Robinson, *An Essay on Marxian Economics*, Chapter V.

Marshall was suspicious of cut-and-dried formulae and approached "the high theme of economic progress"[1] with diffidence and caution, but he seems on the whole to support the view that a rapid rate of saving tends to depress the rate of interest (which he identifies with the rate of profit) by increasing the total stock of capital relatively to the demand for it.

In Keynes' short-period theory, investment is always bringing itself to an end because investment takes place in a boom; a high rate of profit is generated by the seller's market while investment goes on, but the increase in productive capacity produced by the investment is tending to bring the seller's market to an end.

When he turns to the long run he thinks of a rate of profit falling to vanishing point, not as a natural tendency in capitalism, but as an objective of deliberate policy.

I feel sure that the demand for capital is strictly limited in the sense that it would not be difficult to increase the stock of capital up to a point where its marginal efficiency had fallen to a very low figure. This would not mean that the use of capital instruments would cost almost nothing, but only that the return from them would have to cover little more than their exhaustion by wastage and obsolescence together with some margin to cover risk and the exercise of skill and judgment. In short, the aggregate return from durable goods in the course of their life would, as in the case of short-lived goods, just cover their labour-costs of skill and supervision.

Now, though this state of affairs would be quite compatible with some measure of individualism, yet it would mean the euthanasia of the rentier, and consequently, the euthanasia of the cumulative oppressive power of the capitalist to exploit the scarcity-value of capital. Interest today rewards no genuine sacrifice, any more than does the rent of land. The owner of capital can obtain interest because capital is scarce just as the owner of land can obtain rent because land is scarce. But whilst there may be intrinsic reasons for the scarcity of land, there are no intrinsic reasons for scarcity of capital. An intrinsic

1 *Principles*, p. 461.

reason for such scarcity, in the sense of a genuine sacrifice which could only be called forth by the offer of a reward in the shape of interest, would not exist, in the long run, except in the event of the individual propensity to consume proving to be of such a character that net saving in conditions of full employment comes to an end before capital has become sufficiently abundant. But even so, it will be possible for communal saving through the agency of the State to be maintained at a level which will allow the growth of capital up to the point where it ceases to be scarce.[1]

If I am right in supposing it to be comparatively easy to make capital-goods so abundant that the marginal efficiency of capital is zero, this may be the most sensible way of gradually getting rid of many of the objectionable features of capitalism. For a little reflection will show what enormous social changes would result from a gradual disappearance of a rate of return on accumulated wealth. A man would still be free to accumulate his earned income with a view to spending it at a later date. But his accumulation would not grow. He would simply be in the position of Pope's father, who, when he retired from business, carried a chest of guineas with him to his villa at Twickenham and met his household expenses from it as required.[2]

Thus the prediction of a falling rate of profit was converted from a nightmare into an agreeable day-dream.

2

When confronted with statistical data, the traditional theories did not show up at all well. For the advanced industrial countries, particularly the United States, the figures appear to show a marked increase (averaging over booms and slumps) in the value of capital per man, with relatively small changes, one way or the other, in the ratio of output to capital or the share of profits in total proceeds. This indicates a more or less constant rate of profit on capital. Technical progress and the availability

[1] *General Theory*, pp. 375–6.
[2] Ibid., p. 221.

of natural resources had evidently been strong enough to make nonsense of predictions based on diminishing returns, rising organic composition or falling marginal productivity.

The weak point in the neo–classical doctrine is that technical progress is treated as an occasional shock which shifts the equilibrium position of the system. Harrod set us off on a fresh line by treating technical progress as a built-in propensity in an industrial economy.

The famous formula, $g = s/v$ — the percentage growth of total income per annum is equal to the proportion of income saved divided by the ratio of capital to annual income — expresses the notion that output per unit of capital can be taken as constant while the stock of capital increases; when employment of labour is not increasing at an equal rate, this means that output per man is increasing as fast as capital per man.

In various versions, the formula for steady growth was set out, apparently quite independently of each other, by Harrod,[1] Domar,[2] and Mahalanobis[3]; they had also a then unknown forerunner in the Soviet economist Fel'dman.[4] Such coincidences (like the coincidence of Kalecki's discovery of Keynes' theory) are an indication that a stage has been reached in the evolution of a subject when there is a particular next step that has to be taken.

The formula shrugged off the burden of traditional assumptions. When inventions, discoveries and improvements in transport open up new sources of raw materials sufficiently fast, there are no diminishing returns. When technical progress is neutral, there need be no rise in organic composition. When

[1] "An Essay in Dynamic Theory," *Economic Journal*, March 1939.

[2] "Capital Expansion, Rate of Growth and Employment," *Econometrica*, April 1946.

[3] "Some Observations on the Process of Growth of National Income," *Sankhya*, September 1953.

[4] "On the Theory of Economic Growth," *Planovoe Khoziaistvo*, November 1928. *See* Domar, *Essays in the Theory of Economic Growth*.

it is sufficiently rapid, there is no fall in marginal productivity. Taking off traditional blinkers, we have wider fields to survey.

The formula has made a great negative contribution to the development of economics; it marks, as it were, the watershed between Keynesian and modern analysis; but regarded as a positive contribution to thought it has not proved so useful.

The formula seems to suggest that the rate of growth of an economy is determined by technical conditions (which within certain limits fix the ratio of capital to income) and the propensity of the population to save. This leaves out of account the most important element in the whole affair — the decisions governing the rate of accumulation of capital.

In a private-enterprise economy decisions to invest are taken in the light of prospective profits, and, as the *General Theory* shows, prospective profits are depressed, not increased, by thrifty individuals refraining from expenditure for consumption. Thrift, in itself, is a deflationary, depressive, factor in a market economy; it is helpful to accumulation only in so far as the propensity to invest is strong enough to be tending to generate inflationary conditions. When the propensity to invest is weak, thrift only makes it all the weaker.[1]

The first question to be discussed in a theory of development under private enterprise should be: What governs the overall rate of accumulation of capital? On this question accepted teaching, still doped by static equilibrium analysis, has very little to say.

In the formal part of Keynes' theory, the rate of investment tends to be such as to bring the marginal efficiency of capital

---

[1] Harrod, of course, intended to emphasize just this point, but he did it in a backforemost way. He takes the rate of profit on capital to be somehow determined by the rate of interest. His "warranted rate of growth" is not the rate of accumulation that firms *want* to carry out at that rate of profit, but the rate they *have* to carry out if that rate of profit is to be realized. The "warranted" rate is higher the greater the propensity to save of the community. Greater thriftiness requires a higher rate of growth, but does not provide any motive for it.

into equality with the rate of interest. This is purely formal. The marginal efficiency of capital means the expected profit to be obtained from an investment, *allowing for risk and uncertainty*. The statement that the marginal efficiency of capital equals the rate of interest then means no more than that the premium for risk is the difference between prospective profits and the relevant rate of interest.

In setting up trade-cycle models it is usual to distinguish "autonomous" investment which is independent of short-term influences from that which is induced by recent changes in the level of income or of profits. For a long-run analysis it is precisely what governs "autonomous" investment that we need to know.

Kalecki postulates that investment plans are limited by finance. Finance is supplied from retained profits of the firms carrying out the investment and from borrowing, which is limited to some coefficient of self-finance. Transposed from his trade-cycle model into a long-run setting, this only shows that investment (in money terms) has inertia; when the rate of investment has been high in the recent past, profits have been high, and funds are available to maintain a high rate of investment. When it has been low, low profits and limited borrowing power keep it low. It does not throw any light on what governs the level of investment in the first place.

Marx exclaims: "Accumulate! Accumulate! That is Moses and the Prophets." Capitalists invest because it is their nature to do so.

Keynes does not take his own formal model seriously —

It is a characteristic of human nature that a large proportion of our positive activities depend on spontaneous optimism rather than on a mathematical expectation, whether moral or hedonistic or economic. Most, probably, of our decisions to do something positive, the full consequences of which will be drawn out over many days to come, can only be taken as a result of animal spirits — of a spontaneous urge to action rather than inaction, and not as the outcome of a weighted average of quantitative benefits multiplied by quantitative probabilities. Enterprise only pretends to itself to be mainly actuated by the statements in its own prospectus, however candid and sincere. Only a little more than an expedition to the South Pole, is it based on an exact calculation of benefits to come. Thus if the animal spirits are dimmed and the spontaneous optimism falters, leaving us to depend on nothing but a mathematical expectation, enterprise will fade and die; though fears of loss may have a basis no more reasonable than hopes of profit had before.[1]

To understand the motives for investment, we have to understand human nature and the manner in which it reacts to the various kinds of social and economic system in which it has to operate. We have not got far enough yet to put it into algebra.

In spite of its weak treatment of the determinants of accumulation, Harrod's model made an important contribution to the argument. It emphasizes the distinction between the rate of accumulation required to realize the "natural" rate of growth, that is to say the *technically possible* rate of growth, and the rate which actually occurs in an unplanned private-enterprise economy.

The "natural" rate of growth is governed by the rate of growth of the labour force (neglecting complications of changing hours of work and so forth) and the rate of growth of output per head (which Harrod takes to be governed by "autonomous" technical progress). His diagnosis is that actual accumulation normally falls short of the rate required to realize the technically possible rate of growth of output. In poor countries, especially when the population is growing rapidly, it is impossible to extract sufficient saving. In wealthy countries, the propensity to invest is too weak.[2]

[1] *General Theory*, p. 161.
[2] This is expressed in Harrod's terminology by a warranted rate of growth—that is a propensity to save—which is too high.

It is evidently an unrealistic simplification to make technical progress completely autonomous. There is a strong connexion between the drive to accumulate and the drive to increase productivity.[1] This adds *a fortiori* force to the argument. When a capitalist economy comes up against a scarcity of labour while the urge to accumulate is strong, it sets about finding labour-saving improvements in methods of production, and, since these apply particularly to the design of equipment, they are just as likely to reduce the capital/income ratio as to raise it. In short, the possible rate of growth is increased by the very fact that the realized rate is high.

The response of technical progress to an excess demand for labour obviously cannot be relied upon to work without limit. The rate of rise of output per head could not be pushed up indefinitely without causing a fall in the rate of profit. But we do not know where the limit lies, for the system has never been pushed up to it for long enough to find out.

On the other tack, it is clear enough that technical progress is not inhibited by a deficiency of demand for labour. The competitive struggle between firms, and the adaptation to industrial use of discoveries made in the cause of science or war, are continually increasing productivity also when there is a surplus of available labour. The failure of the actual rate of growth to keep up with the "natural" rate then appears in the guise of technological unemployment.

Harrod's analysis of the relations between the actual accumulation of capital and the accumulation required to realize the maximum rate of growth compatible with a constant level of the rate of profit, interpreted in this way, opens up many

[1] This is emphasized by Kaldor (*Essays on Economic Stability and Growth*, p. 267) but unfortunately he makes the rate of technical progress (shown by the height of his technical-progress curve) autonomous and allows only the degree of bias in the capital-using or capital-saving direction (shown by a point on the curve) to be influenced by the rate of accumulation (shown by the value of $x$ in the diagram).

interesting lines of inquiry. In particular, the tendency to stagnation as it is emerging once more in the United States, can be seen to be due, not to any failure of real resources to expand because of the "closing of the frontier," far less to the saturation of real needs, but to the failure of industry to keep the offer of employment expanding as fast as the labour force.

These lines of inquiry have been very little followed up, perhaps because they lead alarmingly away from the beaten track of equilibrium analysis.

### 3

The search for a theory of accumulation has revived interest in the question of the origins of industrial capitalism, which used to be discussed in terms of Weber's theory of the economic influence of Protestantism (Sombart's theory that it was all due to Catholicism never had much of a run).[1]

Walt Whitman Rostow[2] made a bold bid to capture the market with the doctrine that industrialization begins as a reaction to national humiliation. There is one case which this fits very well — the Meiji Restoration in 1867 in Japan. It does not explain why the reaction in China had to wait till 1949. Moreover the humiliation that Japan was reacting against was the impact of capitalism itself. The discovery that there were in the world peoples whose wealth and power were based on industrial techniques caused Japan, so to say by an act of national will, to master the techniques and push herself into the ranks of power. This type of reaction may explain the spread of capitalism, but not its origins. To attribute the Industrial Revolution to the humiliation of England by van Tromp is altogether too far-fetched.

There is a less well-known theory that seems more promising.

[1] *Der Bourgeois*, Chap. XIX.
[2] *The Stages of Economic Growth.*

This is put forward by a disciple of Veblen, Professor C. E. Ayres.[1] He poses the question: "Why did the industrial revolution occur in Western Europe and in modern times? Why not in China, or in ancient Greece."[2]

What is it in the culture-history of western Europe that is unique? This region was the residuary legatee of thousands of years of civilization in the Mediterranean area, but so were many others. The Nile and Mesopotamian valleys are still inhabited. Wherein does western Europe differ from them?[3]

He finds the answer in the fact that western Europe was the "frontier region of Mediterranean civilization."

A frontier is a penetration phenomenon. It is a region into which people come from another and older center of civilization, bringing with them the tools and materials of their older life, their cereal plants and vines and fruit trees, their domestic animals and accoutrements, their techniques of working stone and wood and their architectural designs and all the rest. They also bring their immemorial beliefs and "values," their mores and folkways. But it is notorious that the latter invariably suffer some reduction in importance under the conditions of frontier life. Existence on the frontier is, as we say, free and easy. Meticulous observance of the Sabbath and the rules of grammar are somehow less important on the frontier than "back home."[4]

He attributes technological progressiveness to the weak hold over society of religion —

The Church must be recognized as the spearhead of institutional resistance to technological change. Under the leadership of the church, feudal society opposed and interdicted all the great innovations of which industrial society is the outgrowth; but that opposition was ineffective — from the point of view of industrial evolution, happily

[1] *The Theory of Economic Progress* (University of North Carolina Press, 1944).
[2] Ibid., p. 129.
[3] Ibid., p. 132.
[4] Ibid., p. 133.

so—and its ineffectiveness was due not to any pronounced difference of temper and intent which might be conceived to distinguish Christianity from other creeds but rather to the fact that it was after all an alien creed which bore much less heavily upon the Western peoples than did Islam upon the Arabs, Hinduism upon India, or Confucianism upon China. When we are tempted to think of the Church as the quintessence of medieval civilization we should stop and ask ourselves which, after all, was the more significant symbol of European culture, Saint Thomas or his contemporary, the Emperor Frederick II? ...[1]

The actual experience of the European peoples was that of a frontier community endowed with a full complement of tools and materials derived from a parent culture and then almost completely severed from the institutional power system of its parent. The result was unique. It is doubtful if history affords another instance of any comparable area and population so richly endowed and so completely severed. That western Europe was the seat of a great civilization in the centuries that followed was due altogether to that endowment no important part of which was ever lost; that it was of all the great civilizations of the time incomparably the youngest, the least rigid, less stifled than any other by age-long accumulations of institutional dust, more susceptible by far than any other to change and innovation, was due to the unique severance. Almost certainly it was this composite character which made the civilization of medieval Europe the parent of industrial revolution.[2]

The great inventions that lead to technical revolutions, in Professor Ayres's view, are essentially new combinations of tools devised for different purposes —

Thus the airplane is a combination of a kite and an internal combustion engine. An automobile is a combination of a buggy with an internal combustion engine. The internal combustion engine itself is a combination of the steam engine with a gaseous fuel which is substituted for the steam and exploded by the further combination of the

[1] Ibid., p. 135.
[2] Ibid., p. 137.

electric spark. This is speaking broadly, of course. In actual practice
the combinations are for the most part much more detailed. What is
presented to the public as a "new" invention is usually itself the
end-product of a long series of inventions. ...[1]

Granted that tools are always tools of men who have the capacity
to use tools and therefore the capacity to use them together, combinations are bound to occur. Furthermore it follows that the more tools
there are, the greater is the number of potential combinations. If we
knew nothing of history but had somehow come to understand the
nature of our tools, we could infer that technological development
must have been an accelerating process, almost imperceptibly slow in
its earlier stages and vertiginously fast in its most recent phase.[2]

The preconditions for the Industrial Revolution were generated
by an accumulation of such combinations. For instance, the
discovery of the New World obviously played a great part in
setting the stage. In Professor Ayres's view, it was the consequence of the development of ocean-going vessels which
resulted from the combination of the Mediterranean with the
Viking traditions of shipbuilding —

The ships which began to cross the oceans toward the end of the
fifteenth century were a combination of these two types. We do not
know exactly how or when or where combination occurred. Perhaps
it was in the shipyards of the coast of the Bay of Biscay, where Viking
culture flowing down met Mediterranean culture flowing up. Even
so, a considerable time elapsed before the meeting was fruitful; but
this may serve to emphasize two points: that the combination was not
deliberate and had no special "end" in view (such as the Indies), and
that a ship is not one simple device but rather a mass of culture traits,
so that combination would almost inevitably be the slow function of a
general cultural amalgamation and general technological development. But it seems to be a fairly safe conjecture that the age of voyage
and discovery was a function of ships, that the ocean-sailing ships

1 Ibid., p. 112.
2 Ibid., p. 119.

were the result of a combination of different types of earlier devices, and that the combination occurred as a result of culture contact.[1]

Once the ships existed, the discoveries were "bound" to occur.

The special characteristic of western Europe was not that such combinations occurred there, for they happen everywhere, but that "ceremonial patterns" of behaviour put up a weaker resistance there, than in the older civilizations, to the spread of new inventions.

This conception throws light on what from some points of view is the outstanding problem of the present day — the relatively slow economic development of India under institutions imitated from parliamentary democracy contrasted with that of China under the direction of the Communist Party. Western liberalism has only warmed the surface of the deep waters of Indian tradition, while in China a violent reversal of ideas has opened the way for rapid changes in technology and in the social forms appropriate to exploiting them.

The closest analogy, however, to the departure of the legions from Britain and Gaul is in Black Africa. Here the most modern technology is coming to the notice of peoples very little encumbered by ancient traditions; if Professor Ayres's theory is correct, they are destined, in due course, to outstrip us all.

4

Of all economic doctrines, the one most relevant to the underdeveloped countries is that associated with Malthus. Not that his theory of population can be applied in any clear way to their problems, but because his very name draws attention to the simple, painful fact that the faster is the growth of numbers the slower is the growth of income per head.

The argument is still often conducted, as it was at first, merely in terms of food supplies. On the one side our flesh is

1 Ibid., p. 143.

made to creep by predictions of mass starvation and on the other we are told what astronomical numbers of bodies could be fed by scientific cultivation of the earth and farming of the sea. Even if the optimistic view turns out to be correct, it is quite beside the point. The point is not what we might be able to do, if we really tried, to output per acre. The point is what we already know that we can do to output per man. The way to raise output per man is through providing equipment and education. In the under-developed countries there are masses of workers employed at a very low level of productivity or scarcely employed at all. To equip and train them for a reasonable level of production is a big job. So long as numbers are growing, the time at which all are equipped is postponed; *a fortiori* the time at which an all-round rise to higher levels of productivity can be set going.

It is true that, with adequate organization, there need be no unemployment, as the Chinese have shown. There is always something useful that can be done even with a man's bare hands. The massive unemployment and under-employment that afflicts the world today shows a defect in social and economic institutions. That is not to say that it is easy to cure. It is far easier to build machines than to reorganize society. The point is that, even if it could be solved, the level of production would remain miserably low. *More* men with *more* bare hands, even if they do not lower the average, make it harder to raise. Granted perfect organization, untrammelled by inappropriate social institutions and operated with probity and wisdom, there is still a limit to the amount of investment that can be carried out by any given labour force (counting exports used to pay for imported equipment as part of investment). The limit is set by the surplus per man employed in producing the mere necessities of consumption over his own consumption. The ratio of the surplus to consumption per man governs the maximum proportion of the labour force that can be allocated to investment.

(This obviously is a crude simplification of an intricate question, but the main principle stands however much it is sophisticated with complexities.)

Now, given the proportion of resources devoted to investment, it is obvious that equipment per head will rise faster the slower the growth in the number of heads. The argument is equally obvious when it is applied to housing and the amenities of towns, and to building up a stock of doctors, teachers, etc., which is by no means the least important part of an investment programme.

The question of population raises so much emotion and touches on such deeply buried complexes that logic plays very little part in the discussion and the above simple point is often overlooked or even denied.

Orthodox Catholicism and orthodox Marxism agree in protesting that there is no such thing as a population problem (though both seem to be softening their attitude a little in recent times). It would be possible to understand the religious argument if it ran thus: "The explosion of population now going on is causing great misery in very many lives, and preventing very many from attaining to modest comfort. But contraception is a sin. It is wrong to help others to commit sins (even when they are not Christians) and avoiding misery is no excuse." Religious people, however, do not generally like to put so high a price on virtue; they prefer to pretend that there is no problem. "With every mouth God sends a pair of hands." True enough, but he does not send a combine-harvester. As for the Marxists, one cannot but suspect that they know better, and have some reason for not saying so.

There is a population problem also in the advanced industrial section of the world. We used to be told that demographic development passes regularly through three stages. First there is a primitive balance of high birth-rate with high death-rate. Then modern improvements in medicine and food supplies reduced the death-rate, and a population explosion occurs. Gradually, with better education, a rise in the proportion of urban to rural population, and a higher standard of life, the birth-rate falls, till a civilized balance is reached. Latter-day experience suggests that, after passing through a low point (at which cries of "Race suicide!" are raised) the birth-rate rises again. We can no longer hope that the mere dissemination of birth-control and family planning is enough to keep numbers in check.

The rise in population in the western world (especially U.S.A.) has set in at a time when technical progress is also rapid. The "natural" rate of growth in Harrod's sense[1] is evidently running ahead of accumulation, and the United States seems to be drifting into a kind of high-level under-development, with employment opportunities falling short of the available labour force. This is mitigated to some extent by a kind of high-level disguised unemployment in small-scale service trades.

The most noticeable effect of a growth in numbers, however, when it occurs at a high standard of life, is the way human beings destroy amenities for each other through cluttering up the country with their bodies, their houses and their motor-cars. The external diseconomies of consumption are then so marked as to leave *utility* theory completely in ruins.

5

In the past, great revolutionary inventions came about accidentally through chance historical events, such as the opening up of communications between Europe and China by the Mongol empire, which led to the adaptation of printing to alphabetic languages.[2] Nowadays research is consciously directed to the solution of technical problems (although unfortunately

[1] *See* p. 107.
[2] Ayres, op. cit., p. 141.

the greater part is devoted to what is euphemistically called defence). The evolution of society also has grown self-conscious. An under-developed country has to take a view about what kind of society it wants to develop.

There are those, still devoted to the doctrines of Adam Smith, who preach to the backward economies that they have only to create favourable conditions for capitalism to blossom and bear fruit. They, for the most part, made sceptical by their own experience, feel that they have waited long enough and demand some quicker-yielding kind of cultivation.

When national authorities take it upon themselves to direct economic development, investment has to be controlled by a conscious plan instead of following the fluctuating animal spirits of private enterprise. Propositions derived from the formula for growth ($g = s/v$) then have something to say. For instance the formula shows that, if a particular rate of growth is to be achieved, the more capital-saving the type of invest-ments to be made, the higher is the ratio of consumption to income that can be permitted (given $g$, a lower value of $v$ entails a lower value of $s$) or that, given the type of investment that is to be undertaken, the rate of growth achieved depends upon the ratio of investment to consumption (given $v$, a higher value of $g$ requires a higher value of $s$).

All the same, the emphasis on saving is more misleading than helpful. The characteristic problem of an under-developed economy is that its present rate of accumulation is too low (in some cases too low even to keep up with the growth of popu-lation, let alone to start reducing under-employment and raising the standard of life). Such economies have before them the heavy task of raising their growth rates, and, however much ingenuity they use in keeping the capital/output ratio down, this must entail (in terms of the formula) an overall rise in the ratio of saving to income. But for the most part, the mass of their people are living below the minimum of subsistence necessary for working efficiency. The problem can be stated in a straight-forward manner in terms of the need to provide for an increase in necessary consumption while restraining unnecessary consumption. The overall saving ratio ($s$ in the formula) distracts attention from the distribution of income between individual families. It helps to disguise the awkward problem of what the Indians have begun to call the "growth of the U-sector," which takes place when private wealth is swollen by the overflow from public investment.

The need to restrain consumption in order to permit the rate of accumulation to increase gives an advantage to the economies carrying out development under socialist institutions. A revolution which nationalizes property without compensation makes resources that formerly fed U-consumption available for investment. The pre-existing surplus of unnecessary consumption is small, however, in relation to the accumulation required. The main advantage of wiping out unearned income is that it makes it easier, morally and politically, to prevent real wages from rising too fast. Moreover collective consumption in the form of medical services, entertainments, and so forth (which are easier to provide in a collectivized economy) contribute more, per unit of national expenditure, to the general welfare (on any reasonable basis of judgment) than a rise of wages spread thinly over individual families.

Marx expected that a socialist revolution would have only to expropriate the expropriators, to take over a highly developed industrial economy as a going concern. As it turns out, socialist economies have to carry out industrialization for themselves, and they have to contend with feudal property relations and ancient ideologies which capitalism failed to break down. The orthodox economist, who cannot approve of socialism or of feudalism either, finds himself sadly bewildered.

Stalin formulated the economic aims of socialism as: "The securing of the maximum satisfaction of the constantly rising material and cultural requirements of the whole society."[1]

Taken positively, this has no more content than any meta-physical slogan; like the slogan "All men are equal," it expresses its point of view through negations. "Constantly rising" requirements means that there is no foreseeable limit to the possible rise in productivity (for, of course, it is not so much the needs as the means to satisfy them that will continually increase). "Cultural" requirements means that growing wealth is not to be confined to physical goods (though these alone enter into the Marxist definition of output). "The whole society" implies a condemnation of the arbitrary distribution of wealth.

There is nothing in this that the orthodox economists can object to. Indeed, it takes the very words out of their mouth. But they were wont to excuse the inequality generated by private property in the means of production because it was necessary to make total income greater. If income grows faster without it, they are in an awkward situation. Perhaps this is why they have crept off to hide in thickets of algebra and left the torch of ideology to be carried by the political argument that capitalist institutions are the bulwark of liberty.


6


Keynes' theory has little to say, directly, to the under-developed countries, for it was framed entirely in the context of an advanced industrial economy, with highly developed financial institutions and a sophisticated business class. The unemployment that concerned Keynes was accompanied by under-utilization of capacity already in existence. It had resulted from a *fall* in effective demand. The unemployment of under-developed economies arises because capacity and effective demand never have been great enough.

[1] *Economic Problems of Socialism in U.S.S.R.*, English edition, p. 45.

All the same, in a negative way the *General Theory* has a great deal to teach.

In particular, it throws light on the meaning of inflation. It was a deeply rooted prejudice in the old teaching, which has by no means been finally weeded out, that inflation is a monetary phenomenon, which can be avoided by a correct manipulation of the supply of currency.

The analysis of the *General Theory* shows that inflation is a real, not a monetary, phenomenon. It operates in two stages (once more giving a crudely simple account of an intricate process). An increase in effective demand meeting an inelastic supply of goods raises prices. When food is supplied by a peasant agriculture a rise of the prices of foodstuffs is a direct increase of money income to the sellers and increases their expenditure. The higher cost of living sets up a pressure to raise wage rates. So money incomes rise all round, prices are bid up all the higher and a vicious spiral sets in.

The first stage — a rise of effective demand — can very easily be prevented by not having any development. But if there is to be development there must be a stage when investment increases relatively to consumption. There must be an increase in effective demand and a tendency towards inflation. The problem is how to keep it within bounds.

Some schemes of investment that seem to be clearly indispensable to improvements in the long run, such as electrical installations, take a long time to yield any fruit and meanwhile the workers engaged on these have to be supplied. The secret of non-inflationary development is to allocate the right amount of quick-yielding, capital-saving investment to the consumption-good sector (especially agriculture) to generate a sufficient surplus to support the necessary large schemes.

It is in this kind of analysis, rather than in the mystifications of "deficit finance," that the clue to inflation is to be found.

The Keynesian analysis also throws light on the question of

the use and abuse of foreign aid. There are two cases in which foreign aid is indispensable to getting development started. The first is when equipment is required which cannot be produced at home at any price, while at the same time world demand for all the commodities that the country can export is inelastic.[1] In such a case no amount of hard work or conscientious absti- nence can make it possible to buy equipment in more than the trickle that limited foreign exchange earnings will pay for.

In the second type of case, the home labour force is technically capable of carrying out the desired investment, but there is no way to procure a sufficient surplus to support men taken from food production to work on investment. In such a case, foreign aid could be used either to import food or to import investment goods. To apply it to the best advantage, it should be allocated in whatever proportions will produce the quickest accumula- tion in the stock of equipment.

Such cases, in strict terms, must be rather rare. Generally, before development has got under way there are some dispens- able imports of consumer goods that could be cut or some dispensable home consumption that could be transmogrified into saleable export goods. Where this hump has not been tapped, foreign aid is not, strictly speaking, indispensable, but it is politically helpful, since it removes the need to cut luxury consumption. When foreign aid is applied to reduction of taxes or takes the form of salaries, commissions and bribes, which are spent on imports that would not have been made without it, it contributes nothing at all to development.

This has now been realized by the U.S. Administration. The members of the Alliance for Progress have been told that aid

---

[1] Inelastic, that is, to a fall in price. It is not common for a country to have a sufficiently reliable monopoly in any exportable to make a rise in price a safe policy. A rise in price, immediately or after an interval, will call rival suppliers into the market or induce buyers to switch their demand to substitutes. A fall in price will be followed by rival sellers. Thus demand may be very elastic to a rise and very inelastic to a fall in price, whatever the initial price may happen to be.

will be given only to honest governments, that have carried out a thoroughgoing land reform and instituted progressive taxes that are actually paid. This ruling seems as though it was inspired by simple faith in economic theory, but no doubt it is not as simple as it seems.

There is another topic, in connexion with problems of underdevelopment, that has been much discussed in terms of theoretical analysis; that is, the choice of technique when a variety of methods are available for the same product. The field is clouded by two opposite prejudices. One is the snob appeal of the latest, most highly automatic equipment and the other the sentimental appeal of the village handicraftsman.

To find a way through the fog, we may first propose two simple rules which appeal to common sense. First, no equipment should be scrapped or methods of production rejected so long as the materials used with them and the labour operating them cannot find a better use elsewhere. The best techniques must be embodied in new investment, but the new does not replace the old; it works beside it. Until all workers are equipped with the best, inferior equipment is better than none. Second, no technique should be chosen just because it gives employment. The object of the operation is not to be able to count up the largest total of statistical employment but to increase production. (It is misleading to state the question in terms of labour-intensive techniques. The advantage of the handicrafts lies in being capital-saving, not in being labour-using.)

There remain cases of genuine doubt where a less capital-using technique, with lower output per head, promises more output per unit of investment, or a quicker return on investment, than another which is more mechanized and requires less labour. It has been argued that in such a case the correct policy is to choose the technique that yields the highest rate of surplus, so as to make the greatest contribution to further accumulation. At first sight this seems very reasonable, since development is the whole object of the operation. But when we look closer, it is not so obvious. The surplus which a technique yields is the excess of net product over the value of the wages of the workers who operate it. A higher surplus means a faster rate of rise in output and employment, starting from a smaller beginning. The more capital-saving technique yields more output and pays more wages. It is for that very reason that it offers a smaller surplus.

There is a choice between some jam today and more jam the day after tomorrow. This problem cannot be resolved by any kind of calculation based on "discounting the future" for the individuals concerned in the loss or gain are different. When the more mechanized, higher-surplus, technique is chosen, the loss falls on those who would have been employed if the other choice had been made. The benefit from their sacrifice will come later and they may not survive to see it. The choice must be taken somehow or other, but the principles of Welfare Economics do not help to settle it.

Indeed, on a high plane of generality there is nothing very much for economic theory to say to the planner, except: Do not listen to those who say you want this rather than that — agriculture, not industry; exports, not home production; light industry, not heavy. You always want both.

Nevertheless, on matters of detail the statistical and mathematical methods evolved by modern economics can be of very great service in the planning of development, provided that they are thoroughly well scrubbed to get the metaphysical concepts cleaned off them.

# VI

## WHAT ARE THE RULES OF THE GAME?

WITH all these economic doctrines, decaying and reviving, jostling each other, half understood, in the public mind, what basic ideas are acceptable, and what rules of policy are derived from them?

I

In the midst of all the confusion, there is one solid unchanging lump of ideology that we take so much for granted that it is rarely noticed — that is, nationalism.

The very nature of economics is rooted in nationalism. As a pure subject it is too difficult to be a rewarding object of study; the beauty of mathematics and the satisfaction of discoveries in the natural sciences are denied to the practitioners of this scrappy, uncertain, ill-disciplined subject. It would never have been developed except in the hope of throwing light upon questions of policy. But policy means nothing unless there is an authority to carry it out, and authorities are national. The subject by its very nature operates in national terms. Marxism also, though theoretically universalist, had to be poured into national moulds when revolutionary administrations were set up. The aspirations of the developing countries are more for national independence and national self-respect than just for bread to eat.

The hard-headed Classicals made no bones about it. They were arguing against the narrow nationalism of Mercantilists in favour of a more far-sighted policy, but they were in favour of Free Trade because it was good for Great Britain, not because it was good for the world.

The neo-classical doctrine purported to be universalist. *Utility* knows no frontiers. When Edgworth proposed to add up units of happiness he proposed that every individual should count for one.[1] He did not say that every Englishman should count for one.

But, as it works out, the very fact that the *utility* doctrine cut across class makes it all the more nationalistic. As Gunnar Myrdal has argued[2] the appeal to national solidarity which supports the Welfare State itself makes solidarity of the human race all the more difficult to achieve.

The neo-classicals' ideology purported to be based on universal benevolence, yet they naturally fell into the habit of talking in terms of National Income and the welfare of the people. Our nation, our people were quite enough to bother about.

Nowadays, a conscientious writer like Professor Meade, before setting out the merits of the free market, is careful to say "In order that the monetary and pricing system should work with equity it is necessary to achieve a fair distribution of income and property" and to point out that inequality makes the system not only inequitable but also inefficient, so that a pre-condition for desiring to preserve it is "to take the radical measures to ensure a tolerably equitable distribution of income and property."[3] But he does not for a moment consider any other distribution than that between the citizens of Great Britain. It seems just as natural as breathing to limit equity and efficiency to our own shores.

The great central doctrine of the neo-classical school — the case for Free Trade — though it is sophistical when it pretends that no *nation* can ever benefit itself by protection, is impregnable when it maintains that no groups of producers can do themselves good by protection except by doing, at least

[1] Cf. p. 67.
[2] See *An International Economy.*
[3] *Planning and the Price Mechanism*, p. 35.

temporarily, harm to others. But the economists did not argue that it is the duty of richer nations to increase the sum of *utility* in the world by subsidizing imports from the poorer ones.

A genuinely universalist point of view is very rare. The nearest we get to it, usually, is to argue that in a generally prosperous world *we* are likely to do better than in a miserable one. The prosperity of others is not desirable for *their* sake, but as a contribution to *our* comfort; when their prosperity seems likely to threaten ours, it is not desirable at all. This seems such a natural way of thinking, so right and proper, that we do not even notice that it *is* a particular way of thinking; we have breathed this air from birth and it never occurs to us to wonder what it smells of.

In recent times the growth of statistics has provided much food for nationalistic ideology. Several "League tables" are published periodically, of average National Income, rate of growth, percentage of saving, productivity, growth of productivity, etc., and we look anxiously at our placing. When the poor old U.K., as often happens, appears rather low, we are filled with chagrin; or else we set about picking holes in the statistics to show that the placing is wrong; or we point to all sorts of unfair advantages that the wretched foreigners have, which make the comparisons misleading.

In a world of international competition there is a solid reason for being anxious to keep up with the growth of productivity in other trading nations; if we lost markets through being undersold we should find it very hard to avoid reducing our consumption, and a cut in national real income is very disagreeable.

The League tables also can be used to show what is possible, so that an observer who wants in any case to advocate, say, more investment, can appeal to them to silence an opponent who is arguing that it just cannot be done.

These are rational uses of the comparisons. But the main appeal of the League tables is much more simply and directly to an instinct for keeping up with the Joneses projected on to the international plane.

International competition and national policy have been a great spur to economic development. Behind the façade of *laisser-faire* theory the governments of all capitalist nations have boosted trade and production, conquered territories and adopted institutions to help their own citizens to gain advantage. Free-Trade doctrine itself, as Marshall shrewdly observed, was really a projection of British national interests.

The enormous strides made by production under the régime of international competition have brought us to the paradoxical situation that we are in today. Never before has communication been so complete. Never before has educated public opinion in every country been so conscious of the rest of the world. Never before was it worth while to think about poverty as a world problem; it is only now that it seems possible, by the application of science to health, birth control and production, to relieve the whole human race from its worst miseries.

Yet never before has so great a proportion of economic energy and scientific study been devoted to means of destruction. We combine doctrines of universal benevolence with the same patriotism that inspired the horsemen of Ghengis Khan.

"When Nature formed mankind for society," as Adam Smith said, she endowed him with some feeling of sympathy with his fellows. Evolution produces a conscience. But biology ceases at the frontier of the tribe. Evolution will not answer the greatest of all moral questions, Who is my neighbour? At this point Humanity must take over from Nature, but it does not show at the moment any signs of doing so.

National patriotism certainly is a great force for good. Up to the frontier it is unifying. It overcomes the sectional patriotism of racial and religious groups and so makes for internal harmony. Marxists regret the extent to which it overcomes class antagonism. But internal neighbourliness is won by projecting aggression outside. Many things that would be considered disgraceful at home are justified in the name of national interest. As Dr. Johnson said, "Patriotism is the last refuge of a scoundrel." We are a very long way from developing a national conscience which would turn patriotism into a desire to behave well. Of course in this country, particularly, we make a great fuss about national conscience, but it consists mainly in insisting upon everyone ascribing our national policy to highly moral motives, rather than in examining what our motives really are. To take a modern example, when the Devlin Report described Nyasaland as a "police state" there was certainly great indignation. But the indignation, for the most part, was not that a British dependency should be in a condition that lent itself to that description, but rather that anyone should be so lost to proper feeling as to use those words about a British dependency.

As individuals, we value people for what they give to the world, not for what they get out of it. We see clearly enough in each other (though not always each in himself) that outward prestige is a poor substitute for inward content. We see that aggression is a sign of weakness and boasting of a lack of self-confidence. Yet greed, vainglory and oppression are quite acceptable in national terms.

It is true that there is a great deal of international economic benevolence being displayed at the present time, but it always has to be justified as a national interest. We help India (as much as we do) not because we want to multiply "units of happiness" by giving starving people a square meal, but because we hope it will keep up the prestige of the West against the Soviet Union. Judging by the Press, when the hunger that is relieved is in China, we are not particularly pleased about it.

The Keynesian revolution broke through the pretended internationalism of Free-Trade doctrines and helped to introduce a genuine internationalism into our thinking. The post-war international agreements, though strongly influenced by Free-

Trade ideals, left escape-clauses for countries suffering from balance of payments difficulties, and for under-developed countries; and they permitted home employment policy to take precedence over international obligations. In principle, though very little has been done about it, regulation of trade in primary commodities is accepted as an objective of policy (though the Free-Trade fanatics still decry it) and when our own balance of payments improves by impoverishing primary producers, at least we recognize that it is nothing to be proud of.

This awareness of the variety of problems that face other nations, and the abandonment of the pseudo-universalist Free-Trade doctrine, is a great advance in enlightenment. It is also a great increase in mental discomfort. Without the anodyne of *laisser faire* the moral problem, on a world scale, stares us in the face.

2

On the home front also we are newly aware of choices that have to be made and newly deprived of simple principles for making them. The ideology of Full Employment as an end in itself is too thin, too easy to see through. The idea that there is a right, natural, indicated, equilibrium relation between investment and consumption; or between home and foreign investment; or between government and private investment; or a right, natural, equilibrium level of real wages, or of the rate of interest, is discredited by the very fact that national employment policy is admitted to be necessary.

In any case, once it is accepted that a "high and stable level of employment" is going to be provided (leaving aside the question of just how high it should be and whether a few wobbles will not be induced to alleviate the stability) then the question of employment as such ceases to be interesting. It was necessary to argue about it only when the official view was that nothing could be done. Now the argument must be about *what* should be done.

The neo-classical heritage still has a great influence, not only on the teaching of economics but in forming public opinion generally, or at least in providing public opinion with its slogans. But when it comes to an actual issue, it has nothing concrete to say. Its latter-day practitioners take refuge in building up more and more elaborate mathematical manipulations and get more and more annoyed at anyone asking them what it is that they are supposed to be manipulating.

In so far as economic doctrines have an influence on the choice of objectives for national policy, on the whole it is obscurantist rather than helpful.

The *utility* concept purports to look behind the "veil of money" but *utility* cannot be measured, while money values can, and economists have a bias in favour of the measurable like the tanner's bias in favour of leather.

The very fallacies that economics is supposed to guard against, economists are the first to fall into. Their central concept, National Income, is a mass of contradictions. Consumption, for instance, is customarily identified with sale of consumers' goods, and a high rate of "consumption" is identified with a high standard of life. But consumption, in the plain meaning of the term, in the sense that it is connected with the satisfaction of natural wants, does not take place at the moment when goods are handed over the counter, but during longer or shorter periods after that event. This time-dimension is completely left out of the figures. It is left out not because anyone denies its importance but because of the mere difficulty of catching it in a statistical net.

Fashion in clothes is a kind of sport where non-material values enter in, though on utilitarian principles the pain of many losers probably outweighs the pleasure of the few winners. However that may be, in goods whose purpose is to provide material satisfaction, durability is a great gain; if the time-dimension of consumption falls as the quantity-dimension of sales rises, it is a serious error to take the latter as a measure of changes in the standard of life.

Again, according to the doctrine of *utility*, goods are assumed to satisfy wants that exist independently of them. It was for this reason that goods were held to be a Good Thing. It is by no means obvious that goods which carry their own wants with them, through cunning advertisement, are a Good Thing. Surely we should be quite as well off without the goods and without the wants? This is the kind of question that, very naturally, is painfully irritating to National-Income statisticians. (National-Income studies are, of course, extremely valuable in their proper sphere, that is, in measuring changes in output, as an indication of business activity, and changes in productivity as a measure of efficiency.)

The great point of the *utility* theory was to answer Adam Smith's question about water and diamonds — to distinguish *total utility* which is supposed to measure satisfaction and *marginal utility* which is measured by price. Marshall's diagrammatic representation of consumer's surplus is bogus, of course — a pseudo-quantitative treatment of something which by its nature cannot be measured. But the idea behind it is based on common sense. The opportunity to buy a commodity, compared with a situation in which it does not exist, may offer an advantage to consumers which is in no way measured by the sums actually spent on it. Yet in National-Income accounting, goods have to be entered in terms of their exchange values, not their *utilities*. This would be a matter only for philosophical speculation were it not that policy is affected by propaganda for the standard of life as it appears in the figures, and there is a continuous and systematic pressure for goods with a sales value against those which are free. The fight that has to be put up, for instance, to keep wild country from being exploited for money profit is made more difficult because its defenders can be represented as standing up for "non-economic" values (which is considered soft-headed, foolish and unpatriotic) though the economists should have been the first to point out that *utility*, not money, is economic value and that the *utility* of goods is not measured by their prices.

The *laisser-faire* bias that still clings around orthodoxy also helps to falsify true values. When Keynes (in his "moderately conservative" mood) maintained that, provided overall full employment is guaranteed "there is no objection to be raised against the classical analysis of the manner in which private self-interest will determine what in particular is produced,"[1] he had forgotten that in an earlier chapter he had written "There is no clear evidence from experience that the investment policy which is socially advantageous coincides with that which is most profitable."[2] At that point he was considering the bias of private enterprise in favour of quick profits. There is a still more funda-mental bias in our economy in favour of products and services for which it is easy to collect payment. Goods that can be sold in packets to individual customers, or services that can be charged for at so much per head, provide a field for profitable enterprise. Investments in, say, the layout of cities, cannot be enjoyed except collectively and are not easy to make any money out of; while negative goods, such as dirt and noise, can be dispensed without any compensation being required.

When you come to think of it, what can easily be charged for and what cannot, is just a technical accident. Some things, such as drainage and street lighting, are so obviously necessary that a modicum is provided in spite of the fact that payment has to be collected through the rates, but it is only the most glaring necessities that are met in this way, together with some tradi-

[1] *General Theory*, pp. 378–9.
[2] Ibid., p. 157.

tional amenities, like flower-beds in the parks, that are felt to be necessary to municipal self-respect.

Funds for investment in profitable concerns are very largely provided out of the profits made on past investments. When we buy a packet of goods we pay the costs of producing it (including a return to the lenders of the finance that has gone into equipment for making it) and a bit extra as well, which goes to undistributed profits to finance more investments. In many cases the price also includes a contribution to taxes to be spent on general administration, social services, interest on the national debt, defence, and so forth. The difference between profit margins and indirect taxes, in terms of their economic functioning, is not at all clear cut; one is no more and no less a "burden" than the other. The difference between them is that the outlay of profit margins on dividends, amenities or profitable investment, under nominal control of the shareholders, is in the hands of boards of directors, while the outlay of rates and taxes is in the hands of city corporations and government departments, under nominal control of the electorate. The idea that one is necessarily more "economic" than the other has no foundation except in ideological prejudice.

Professor Galbraith depicts the situation in America, where both the output of saleable goods and the neglect of non-saleable services are even more extreme than here —

The family which takes its mauve and cerise, air-conditioned, power-steered, and power-braked car out for a tour passes through cities that are badly paved, made hideous by litter, blighted buildings, bill-boards, and posts for wires that should long since have been put underground. They pass on into a countryside that has been rendered largely invisible by commercial art. (The goods which the latter advertise have an absolute priority in our value system. Such aesthetic considerations as a view of the countryside accordingly come second. On such matters we are consistent.) They picnic on exquisitely packaged food from a portable icebox by a polluted stream and go on to spend the night at a park which is a menace to public health and morals. Just before dozing off on an air-mattress, beneath a nylon tent, amid the stench of decaying refuse, they may reflect vaguely on the curious unevenness of their blessings.[1]

We have not quite reached that stage here, but we are well on the way.

Some interpretations of employment policy take it for granted that private enterprise investment should always be given the first claim on resources and public investment should take up the slack. Thus "public works" should be undertaken when private investment appears to be going into a slump and slackened off again when private investment picks up.

It was all very well for Lloyd George and Keynes to advocate clearing the slums and widening the roads purely as a means of giving work, because the official orthodoxy was opposed to doing anything, but now it does not seem to make much sense that we have to wait for a slump to get these jobs done. It is possible to argue that private investment is helpful to exports, that we cannot afford to clear the slums until our industry is in better shape, and that exports cannot flourish unless profitable industry as a whole is flourishing. That is a logical argument though not necessarily convincing. But the argument that public investment, however beneficial, must be less eligible from a national point of view than any private investment, merely because it is public, has no logical basis; it is just a hang-over from *laisser-faire* ideology.

To take another example, Keynes, as we saw[2] maintained (when he allowed his mind to stray over long-run problems) that investment steadily maintained at full-employment levels would soon saturate all useful demands for capital equipment, and require a reduction of the rate of interest to vanishing point. But he did not lament it; he looked forward to it as the begin-

<hr />

[1] *The Affluent Society*, pp. 186–7.
[2] See above, p. 103.

ning of an age of civilized life. The "vulgar Keynesians" took it up in another sense. They turned the prospective drying up of profitable investment opportunities into the "stagnation thesis." The stagnationists, instead of welcoming the prospect of a period when saving would have become unnecessary, high real wages would have reduced the rate of profit to vanishing point, and technical progress could be directed to lightening toil and increasing leisure, regard its approach as a menace. This, of course, is a perfectly reasonable point of view if the aim of economic life is held to be to provide a sphere for making profits. Satiation of material wants is bad for profits. But this does not go very well with the usual claim that the private enterprise system is justified by its power to meet wants.

In practice employment policy is not based on any particular theory but follows the line of least resistance. Public investment is the easiest thing to cut when restriction appears to be called for, and private consumption the pleasantest thing to boost when a stimulus is needed. From the point of view of planning socially beneficial investment it is usually: Heads I win and tails you lose.

Not only is the system distorted by its bias towards investing in what happens to be profitable, but even within that sphere there is no reason to expect the profit motive to lead to a well balanced pattern of investment. This has always been a weak point in the neo-classical system. The doctrine that, under conditions of free competition, given resources are used to yield maximum satisfaction, applies essentially to an equilibrium position. It can be demonstrated only by assuming that an equilibrium exists and showing that a *departure* from it would be harmful (it also has to assume, of course, that the distribution of income is somehow what it ought to be). Walras had the ingenious idea of making the inhabitants of his market "shout" their offers until the equilibrium has been found, and then start actual trading at the equilibrium prices. It is pure effrontery to extend this kind of equilibrium conception to investment; an equilibrium pattern of investment worked out on this system is possible only in a fully planned economy (if there).

Marshall is less fanciful; he assumes that there is a general equilibrium level of profits, and that each particular industry is attracted to invest faster when profits are higher than normal, and so bring down the prices of its products by increasing the supply. But in Vol. I of the *Principles* he assumes general equilibrium conditions and studies departure from equilibrium in one industry at a time. He never got round to writing the volume that would explain how general equilibrium was preserved.

And his own argument shows that it will not be. His own argument shows that a competitive industry will overshoot the equilibrium point under the influence of the prospect of super-normal profits and fall into a period of sub-normal profits thereafter. This arises out of the very nature of competition. Each firm in a seller's market aims to expand its own productive capacity up to the point that would be profitable if the seller's market were to last, but the others are doing the same, and the seller's market will not last. Even a general knowledge that this is likely to be so does not stop the overshoot, for each hopes to be among the lucky ones who will survive while the coming buyer's market drives *others* out of existence.

By the same token, where an industry is in control of a monopoly, wise planning for the future dictates reserve in responding to an increase in demand. Surplus capacity is the great evil to be avoided. The stronger the monopoly, the more cautious it will be, and if, by always remaining in the rear of demand, it can make a seller's market permanent, so much the better.

In a world in which some industries are much easier to enter than others, there is a systematic distortion in the pattern of investment, which is something over and above the general instability that employment policy is designed to control, over and above mistakes in forecasting which are liable to occur in any system, and over and above the misdirection of investment through speculative influences, which Keynes referred to when he said that "When the capital development of a country becomes a by-product of the activities of a Casino, the job is likely to be ill done."[1]

3

All this would be true even if the distribution of income and wealth were accepted as fair and reasonable. In a modern democracy that is far from being the case. Through political channels — the tax system and social services — we are continually pushing against the distribution of income that our economic system throws up.

The pressure is haphazard and often ineffective (the difference between our highly progressive tax system on paper and our highly regressive system of tax avoidance in reality is sufficiently notorious). The effort at redistribution has no particular philosophy behind it and there does not seem to be any rational criterion for the point at which to draw the line; it sways to and fro (though not very far) as the balance of political pressures shifts.

The *utility* economists, according to Wicksell, were committed to a "thoroughly revolutionary programme" precisely on this question of distribution of income.[2] Marshall, and to some extent Pigou, got out of the fix that their theory had landed them in by emphasizing the danger to total physical national income that would be associated with an attempt to increase its *utility* by making its distribution more equal. This argument has been spoiled by the Keynesian revolution. If, as Keynes expected, saving is more than sufficient for a satisfactory

[1] *General Theory*, p. 159.
[2] Cf. p.53.

rate of private investment, to use it for social purpose is not only harmless but actually beneficial to National Income, while if more total saving is needed than would be forthcoming under *laisser faire* it can easily be supplemented by budget surpluses.

Edgworth, as we saw above,[1] and many after him, took refuge in the argument that we do not really know that greater equality would promote greater happiness, because individuals differ in their capacity for happiness, so that, until we have a thoroughly scientific hedonimeter, "the principle 'every man, and every woman, to count for one,' should be very cautiously applied."[2]

Many years ago, this point of view was expressed by Professor Harberler: "How do I know that it hurts you more to have your leg cut off than it hurts me to be pricked by a pin?" It seemed at the time that it would have been more telling if he had put it the other way round.

Such arguments are getting rather dangerous nowadays, for though we shall presumably never have a hedonimeter whose findings would be unambiguous, the scientific measurement of pain is fairly well developed, and it would be very surprising if a national survey of the distribution of susceptibility to pain turned out to have just the same skew as the distribution of income.

If the question is once put: Would a greater contribution to human welfare be made by an investment in capacity to produce knick-knacks that have to be advertised in order to be sold or an investment in improving the health service? it seems to me that the answer would be only too obvious; the best reply that *laisser-faire* ideology can offer is not to ask the question.

It is possible to defend our economic system on the ground that, patched up with Keynesian correctives, it is, as he put it,

---

[1] See p. 67.
[2] *Mathematical Psychics*, p. 81.

the "best in sight." Or at any rate that it is not too bad, and change is painful. In short, that our system is the best system that we have got.

Or it is possible to take the tough-minded line that Schumpeter derived from Marx. The system is cruel, unjust, turbulent, but it does deliver the goods, and, damn it all, it's the goods that you want.

Or, conceding its defects, to defend it on political grounds — that democracy as we know it could not have grown up under any other system and cannot survive without it.

What is not possible, at this time of day, is to defend it, in the neo-classical style, as a delicate self-regulating mechanism, that has only to be left to itself to produce the greatest satisfaction for all.

But none of the alternative defences really sounds very well. Nowadays, to support the *status quo*, the best course is just to leave all these awkward problems alone.

4

To descend from questions of universal and of national policy to the internal operation of the system, let us ask what rules of the game are accepted nowadays for various players in an industrial economy.

What about Trade Unions? According to strict *laisser-faire* doctrine they used to be placed on a par with monopolies. The free operation of market forces would secure for each group of workers their marginal net product, and a Trade Union, by forcing the wage above its equilibrium level, would cause unemployment, just as a monopolist restricts sales by keeping up prices.

In some ways the most striking novelty in Keynesian doctrine was that (abstracting from effects on foreign trade) an all-round reduction in wages would not reduce unemployment and (introducing Kalecki's elaboration) would actually be likely to increase it.

At the same time "imperfect competition" had come into fashion and discredited the idea that market forces can be relied upon to establish the equality of wages with the value of marginal products, so that even on its own waters the old orthodoxy could not keep afloat.

Nowadays it is pretty generally agreed that Trade Unions do not introduce an element of monopoly into the system but constitute rather what Professor Galbraith[1] has christened a "countervailing power" to cancel the element of monopoly which inevitably exists on the employer's side of the wage bargain. At the same time the employer's side, at least in big business, has learned to accept the Trade Unions and on the whole, apart from occasional flurries, to co-exist with them fairly amicably.

The new doctrine, however, cuts both ways. A rising tendency of money wage rates is necessary to keep monopoly in check, but if it goes too fast it does no good to the workers and is a great nuisance to everyone else.

Experience of the vicious spiral in the years of high employment has demonstrated this clearly enough, as an overall truth. But it remains the duty of each Trade Union individually to look after the interests of its own members. To appeal to any one Union to exercise public spirit and refrain from wage demands is appealing to it to betray its trust. An appeal to organized labour as a whole to exercise restraint is naturally regarded with the deepest suspicion as long as profits are not restrained.

Here there has been a spectacular breakdown in the doctrine that the pursuit of self-interest by each promotes the good of all.

The old theory *assumed* full employment and stable prices.

[1] See *American Capitalism*.

Now history has called its bluff. Where is the mechanism that will establish such a situation? The old rules of the game have become unplayable and badly need to be revised.

What about the other side of the bargain? Is it the proper thing for employers to resist wage demands? Not long ago a lockout in the printing trade reduced the British Press to silence, played havoc with publishing business and ruined a number of small local printers. Afterwards the employers claimed credit for having saved the public, at serious loss to themselves, from the greater rise in wages that they would have had to concede if they had settled without a fight.[1] Do we agree in feeling grateful and congratulating them on their public spirit? or do we regret the loss of production and the general ill-will that followed the dispute? Orthodox doctrine cannot help us.

And what about prices? The old theory that they are settled by competition could not survive the long buyer's market of the inter-war period, and the theories of imperfect and monopolistic competition have left mere chaos in their wake. The business man's theory (which has been taken up by some economists) that prices are governed by costs is no more helpful; it is quite impossible to define the cost, including a proper contribution to overheads, depreciation and "a fair and reasonable profit," for any particular batch of output of any particular commodity. Some formula or other for allocating costs can be found that will justify any price, within reason, that a firm finds it convenient to charge.

The businessman's theory, in any case, is evidently not intended to be taken literally, for, with a few exceptions, they do not show any alacrity in reducing prices when costs fall.

All that orthodox theory tells us is that in conditions of perfect competition prices fall with costs and that in conditions of oligopoly they very likely do not. Does theory tell us that it

[1] See *The Times*, 1st September 1959. Letter from J. Brooke-Hunt.

would be a Good Thing if firms acted *as though* there was perfect competition, and brought prices down? This was the view taken (with some hesitation) in the third report of the Cohen Council.[1] It was greeted by business commentators with some surprise. Surely the proper objective in industry is to make profits? There may be cases where a reduction of price will increase profits, and then it is indicated, but the doctrine that prices ought to fall just because costs have come down seemed very odd. A spokesman of the Federation of British Industries, commenting on the Report remarks —

> There are ambiguities in its suggestion that industry should reduce prices. It is one thing to reduce prices and thereby expand demand and output; it is another to hold prices below their market level with the object of curbing profits or dividends.[2]

Then again, there is the question of the durability of commodities, referred to above. Suppose that a manufacturer has discovered a way, without extra cost, to make his products more durable. Should he adopt this method, so as to benefit his customers, or should he rather consider the danger of satisfying their demands and reducing the market for replacements? Would he not be well advised to turn his research workers on to find a less durable material, provided that it can be made to look as attractive and is not much more costly? Here the doctrine that the most profitable is the most socially beneficial course of conduct hits an awkward snag.

Then again, what about dividend policy? There is a strong propensity in human nature, which has not been explained (perhaps a clue might be found in the instincts of animals that live in packs) for the individual to cotton on to any kind of group of which he finds himself a member, and to develop patriotism for it.

[1] Council on Prices, Productivity and Incomes, 1959.
[2] Report in *The Times*, 7th August 1959.

Nation, race, church, city, evoke loyalty. Marx never got round to writing the chapter on class. Class loyalty, in vulgar Marxism, is presented as a form of egoism, but it is not so; it often demands the sacrifice of the immediate interest of an individual.

This tendency of attachment is the foundation for public-school spirit and regimental morale. It also operates strongly for firms; the main cause that has falsified Adam Smith's prediction that joint-stock enterprise would be impossible,[1] and Marshall's dictum that limited liability companies stagnate,[2] is this capacity for managers and boards of directors to project their egos into the organization that they happen to belong to and care for it just as much as if it were a family business.

The entity which evokes this loyalty is the firm as such. The shareholders (apart from those foundation members who are identified with the firm) are regarded more or less on a par with creditors and it is a disagreeable necessity to part with the firm's earnings to satisfy them.

Devotion to the firm as such points to a high rate of self-financing, except in the case of boards of very large companies which want from time to time to make big new issues. They pay out dividends, and seek to keep up the market price of shares, not because they are acting in the interests of the share-holders, but because this is the best way to raise more capital for the firm that they serve.

On this question of distributing profits, what is proper behaviour? Some economists are against self-finance because it spoils the marginal theory. Investment goes where profits happen to have been earned and investments of a relatively low marginal productivity may be pushed by old firms while new ones with very high marginal productivity cannot get finance. Much better, they argue, to distribute profits and let all firms go

---

[1] *Wealth of Nations*, Vol. I, p. 229.
[2] *Principles*, p. 316.

to the market. But of money that has once been paid out, perhaps 10 per cent will be saved and made available for re-investment, whereas 100 per cent of retained profits are re-invested. Is the superior quality of external finance great enough to outweigh such a large difference in quantity?

Management (for Management with a large M is also an entity with its own point of view) is all against this doctrine and regards re-investment as the main justification for profits. The idea that the motive for industry is the pursuit of profit is resented as a dastardly slander. It is quite the other way round: industry is the motive for the pursuit of profit.

In a now forgotten manifesto signed by a hundred and twenty business men, which was issued during the war, we find this credo set forth: Industry (Industry with a big I) —

has a three-fold public responsibility, to the public which consumes its products, to the public which it employs, and to the public which provides the capital by which it operates and develops. ... The responsibility of those directing Industry is to hold a just balance between the varying interests of the public as consumers, the staff and workmen as employees, and the stockholders as investors, and to make the highest possible contribution to the well-being of the nation as a whole.[1]

This sounds pompous and arrogant. Who gave these fellows the right to determine the distribution of the National Income and what super-human wisdom do they claim directs them to distribute it aright? Yet there is a great deal of truth in the view that the power to allocate resources and distribute income has in fact been placed in their hands. To the list of interests which they have to balance should be added, first of all, boards of directors, and secondly, in a vague and more diffused way, that solidarity with their colleagues in an industry which nowadays so much softens the edge of competition, and solidarity with Industry as such — that is with the class to which they belong.

[1] *A National Policy for Industry*, 1942.

But the high-mindedness is not all just a publicity stunt to recommend their class to the rest of us. There is a large element, in the patriotism which attaches a manager to his firm, of a desire for a good reputation and a good conscience. Even when it is hypocritical, hypocrisy — the homage which vice pays to virtue — is much to be preferred to cynicism. The modern capitalist is hardly recognizable in Marx's portrait of the ruthless exploiter, squeezing every drop of surplus out of the sweat of the workers.

Keynes in one of his optimistic moods spoke of the tendency of big business to socialize itself.[1] Nowadays Management (the kind with a big M) likes to see itself as a kind of public service.

All this has been much damaged lately by a violent kick-back of old-fashioned profit-seeking capitalism. The legal fiction that firms belong to their shareholders has been taken up to knock high-minded, gentlemanly Management over the head. Once more some economists, clinging to the old orthodoxy, welcome the take-over bidder on the grounds that what is profitable must be right, conceding to the profits of financial manipulations the halo that once belonged to the "reward of Enterprise." Those who hold that the proper purpose of industry is to pay dividends must welcome the pressure being put upon boards of directors to offer counter-bribes to their shareholders.

Which side should we be on? Is the gentlemanly public spirit of Management too often a cloak for gentlemanly ease and long week-ends? Will the exaltation of the shareholder make managers cynical and Trade Unions aggressive, and face us once more with sharp questions which have been muffled in the comfortable woolly-mindedness of the Welfare State?

Another question on which orthodoxy has led us into great confusion is monopoly. Generally, in the orthodox scheme, monopoly is a Bad Thing. Professor Knight has been known to

[1] *Essays in Persuasion*, p. 314.

attack the U.S. anti-trust laws as an illegitimate interference with the freedom of the individual, but for most economists competition is absolutely essential to the justification of *laisser faire*; it is competition which equates the margins, distributes resources so as to maximize *utility* and generally makes the whole scheme work.

But competition, surely, is the main cause of monopoly? How can it be that to lower prices, expand markets, undersell rivals, is a Good Thing, but that the firm that succeeds in overcoming these difficulties and remains in possession of the field is a wicked monopolist? The objection to restrictive practices, and the main justification for the present campaign against them, is that they restrain competition and keep inefficient producers going. If the campaign succeeds, competition, driving out the inefficient, will create more monopolies. Is that what we want? And if not, what *do* we want? What are the rules of the game?

5

Perhaps all this seems negative and destructive. To some, perhaps, it even recommends the old doctrines, since it offers no "better 'ole" to go to. The contention of this essay is precisely that there is no "better 'ole."

The moral problem is a conflict that can never be settled. Social life will always present mankind with a choice of evils. No metaphysical solution that can ever be formulated will seem satisfactory for long. The solutions offered by economists were no less delusory than those of the theologians that they displaced.

All the same we must not abandon the hope that economics can make an advance towards science, or the faith that enlightenment is not useless. It is necessary to clear the decaying remnants of obsolete metaphysics out of the way before we can go forward.

The first essential for economists, arguing amongst themselves, is to "try very seriously," as Professor Popper says that natural scientists do, "to avoid talking at cross purposes" and, addressing the world, reading their own doctrines aright, to combat, not foster, the ideology which pretends that values which can be measured in terms of money are the only ones that ought to count.

# INDEX OF REFERENCES